A HUNGER *for* THE HOLY

NURTURING INTIMACY *with* CHRIST

CALVIN MILLER

WITH LEARNING ACTIVITIES BY DALE MCCLESKEY

Lifeway Press®
Nashville, Tennessee

ISBN 0-6330-9934-1

This book is a resource in the Personal Life category of the Christian Growth Study Plan.
Course CG-1024

Dewey Decimal Classification: 248.84
Subject Headings: SPIRITUAL LIFE

Editor-in-Chief: Dale McCleskey
Art Director: Jon Rodda
Copy Editor: Connie Eubanks

To order additional copies of this resource: WRITE LifeWay Church Resources Customer Service; One LifeWay Plaza; Nashville, TN 37234-0113; FAX order to (615) 251-5933; PHONE (800) 458-2772; E-MAIL to *customerservice@lifeway.com;* ORDER ONLINE at *www.lifeway.com;* or VISIT the LifeWay Christian Store serving you.

Printed in the United States of America

Leadership and Adult Publishing
LifeWay Church Resources
One LifeWay Plaza
Nashville, TN 37234-0175

Table of Contents

Dedication

To Barbara, my lifetime companion. You make everything worthwhile better and everything else bearable.

Acknowledgement

My heartfelt thanks to Dale McCleskey, an editor whose hunger for the holy becomes a passion for excellence in these pages.

About the Author

Calvin Miller, professor of preaching and personal studies at Samford University in Birmingham, Alabama, received his D.M. from Midwestern Baptist Theological Seminary and has served on the editorial boards of such publications as *Leadership* and *Preaching* magazines. An accomplished author of more than forty books—including the popular Singer trilogy, *The Unchained Soul*, *Once Upon a Tree*, and *The Book of Jesus*—Calvin Miller brings an awe-inspiring artistry to the craft of writing.

Introduction

Christ's table is made elegant by its simplicity. It has but two chairs, two place cards. Beside one place is a card that reads "Jesus." By the other is a card marked with your name. A candle burns from the table's center, ready to cast its amber enchantment on both your eager faces.

Across the years I have come to delight in the fellowship of the wilderness table. The meal itself is a banquet of substance. Holiness is the fare. Union with Christ is the point of the occasion. He knows I have a terrible craving for His presence. I know that He longs to see teacher and pupil made one by their common appetite for togetherness.

And I am hungry!
Hungry for the Holy.
The table is prepared.
I take my chair.
I wait.

Welcome to the group study of *A Hunger for the Holy*. Here I want to bring together two almost-opposite elements of the Faith. We each relate to Christ individually. We meet with Him alone or we don't meet Him at all. Yet our relationship screams for community. So this book is designed for a daily time alone with Christ and His Word. It also provides for a weekly gathering of believers for encouragement and shared experience.

Though you can study this book without the videos, I hope you can access the leader kit. In it you will find a movie called *The Psalmist* that I wrote to go along with the study. Show the movie to your church or Bible study group. Then meet each week with a small group as you study the Psalms together. Each week I will meet with you through the video segments to begin your study.

My prayer for you is that you will benefit from a daily time with the ultimate author of the Psalms. The table awaits. Your place is set.

WEEK 1

HUNGERING AFTER THE HOLY LIFE

DAY 1 THE JOURNEY INWARD

Blessed is the man who does not walk in the counsel of the wicked or stand in the way of sinners or sit in the seat of mockers.—Psalm 1:1

We humans are a hungry lot. A hunger to know who we are drives us, yet our identity is embedded in the heart of the Holy God. Unless we dig into the epicenter of heaven, we will be forever condemned to walk the arid edges of self-understanding.

We shrink to step across the threshold and invite God in, yet we do not hesitate to stick our hands into the human throng and shake a thousand others. No matter how we love our noisy and hurried lives, the fast-action theater at last empties out, and we find ourselves in lonely cells of bulky silence that compels us to turn and face our inner selves—and our Mighty God.

When you are able to create a lonely place in the middle of your actions and concerns, your successes and failures slowly can lose some of their power over you.
Henri J. M. Nouwen

Galileo: I'm not a theologian: I'm a mathematician.
Sagredo: You are a human being! [Almost shouting] Where is God in your system of the universe?
Galileo: Within ourselves. Or—nowhere.
Bertolt Brecht

What three life experiences have most made you face your inner self?

- ❑ a death
- ❑ a physical limitation
- ❑ a relationship
- ❑ family responsibilities
- ❑ an illness
- ❑ a sense of God's majesty
- ❑ a disappointment
- ❑ an act of service
- ❑ a failure
- ❑ other______________

We instantly turn from inwardness, for it seems a kind of nakedness and soul exposure. Self simpers where none can see. Outwardly it pretends to be gallant or holy, while inwardly it is aware of its insecurity and corruption.

The journey inward is painful. Remember Hamlet forcing his mother to grapple with her inner wickedness: "Come, come, and sit you down; you shall not budge. You go not till I set you up a glass where you may see the inmost part of you."[1] The young prince forced his mother to stare at the hidden woman who skulked at the center of her being. The question is, what did Gertrude see? What of our own inner selves does God's glass reflect?

Describe in single words what you think you would see if God gave you a glimpse of your own inmost self.

____

____

Many Bible passages (such as Luke 13:3 or Acts 2:38) issue a call for repentance. Repentance? The very word stops our hearts with chilling honesty, for it insists that we come clean with God before we make life's important choices. Repentance demands that we choose a path of holy living.

The psalmist defines the paths we must avoid as we dare to journey inward. Repentance grows from those altars which call for the bold disclosure of our inward selves to our loving Father. But what is the best definition of repentance?

How would you define repentance?

____

____

____

In repentance we stand together with Christ as we look inward and throw even the darkest fissures of our souls beneath God's certain light. The Greek word for repentance is *metanoeo*. It comes from two words meaning change and mind. Thus it means, to change our attitude, thoughts, and behaviors concerning the demands of God.

Repentance is both an action and a condition. As an action it is both something we do and something God does to us because alone we cannot change. Our repentance must grow as our understanding of and relationship with Christ grows. We discover more or ourselves that must be brought to God.

I remember that night so long ago when, as a boy, I asked the living Christ to enter my life. Suddenly, even as a child, I knew the pain of Hamlet's reflecting glass. But the pain soon left, and in its place was born the radiant reality of Christ's indwelling.

But the pain soon left, and in its place was born the radiant reality of Christ's indwelling.

At what age did you first experience repentance?

How was your "mind changed" by your encounter with God?

How is your repentance today different than when you were a young Christian?

I remember the frustration of trying to tell my friends about the inward Christ who had replaced my guilt and self-recriminations with His glorious affirmation. I could tell by the way others looked at me that they could not understand God's invasion into my life. Yet I wanted everyone to know. I tried to tell my family, but they, too, greeted me with quizzical expressions. I suddenly saw that the Christ who had taken up residence inside me was too inward to be explained outwardly. I could not make Him big enough to portray His inner glory to others. On the other hand, the world beyond me could not make Him small enough to fit in its smaller, more cramped understanding of God.

Check any of the experiences described in the last paragraph with which you identify.

- ❑ guilt replaced by a sense that God accepted me
- ❑ friends who couldn't understand
- ❑ a desire to share Jesus' love with others
- ❑ family members who also couldn't understand
- ❑ frustration with a world that insists on a cramped understanding of God

How was your experience different from that of the author?

So, even at an early age, I learned that life in Christ defies externalization. The historical facts surrounding Christ are both outward and clear. Certainly the theological truths are sure. Yet the reality of Jesus is always a matter of the heart. The fullness of His great love defies definition, and yet salvation spills over the edges of our most private selves.

Day 2 THE DELIGHTS OF INWARDNESS

His delight is in the law of the LORD, and on his law he meditates day and night.—Psalm 1:2

Yesterday we began to explore both the Psalms and the issue of our inner life in Christ. Please take time to slowly and reflectively read all of the first Psalm.

What would you say was the greatest desire of the writer of Psalm 1?

____

____

To covet God's holiness is a righteous coveting. To lust for godliness is a glorious passion. But the straining for the holiness suggested by the Psalm brings out the same frustrations I felt as a child. By what path do we arrive there? How can I tell you? How shall I define it?

Inwardness defies all laws of space and time and endows us with a life and destiny too great to be our own. What we contain is more than what we are. For this indwelling Christ brings with Him a love beyond dimension; yet for all its vastness, it chooses to make its throne our fleshly frame. With Him comes His cosmic size, poured unexplainably into the thimble-like containers of our souls.

Dream for a moment. What would your life be like if Psalm 1 truly described you through and through?

____

____

____

What problems that trouble you would be diminished?

____

____

____

What priorities in your life would be changed?

____

____

____

Why is God's law so delightful? It reveals God's very heart to us. It delivers us into a new intimacy with Christ. This new intimacy is a wonderful soul-to-soul life nurtured by the Savior in the very bosom of God. Only there—in the inward places, where our souls merge—do we find the epicenter of meaning.

Carefully consider what the following story says about inwardness.

A contemporary philosopher often spoke of "the very center of the very center." His daughter once complained that she could see only the outside of things. Since they were enjoying some fruit at the time, the father grabbed a knife and cut a grape in half. "Can you see the inside now?" he asked her. His daughter now felt she was seeing the inside of the grape, but the father said, "No, this is not the inside of the inside. It is only the outside of the inside." To see the "inside of the inside," he told her, he would have to cut the grape halves into quarters.

He did this. "Is this the inside?" he asked. Again she felt she was seeing the inside. But her father told her that she was still not seeing the inside. However hard the philosopher attempted to open the center of the grape, he only succeeded in creating new "outsides" by driving the "inside" further in.

Write a moral for the father-daughter experiment with the grape. Plan to share your statement with your group this week.

____

____

How do you think we evangelicals tend to rate in the balance between inwardness and outward expressions of the faith?

overstress the outward ——————————————— overstress the inward

Which description would best fit your spiritual life?

- ❑ I ignore the inward for the outward.
- ❑ I over emphasize the inward.
- ❑ I think I pretty much balance the two.

Discussing inwardness does not define it, and exposing it is impossible. We can never truly locate it. Does it reside in the mind or in the heart? What is the difference between the two? Evangelicals teach their children to "invite Jesus into their hearts." We teach those same children to sing:

Into my heart, into my heart,
Come into my heart, Lord Jesus.
Come in today. Come in to stay.
Come into my heart, Lord Jesus.[2]

A thousand other such songs and prayers pay tribute to the delight of knowing God. All of them are scored to praise the path of inwardness. Too often, we champion the kind of faith that emphasizes logic or theological discussion at the expense of feeling. Then we become like the Tin Man in *The Wizard of Oz,* who believed all his problems would be solved if he only had a heart.

What happens if our relationship with God becomes all a matter of the intellect?

- ❑ We may become heartless truth-detectors like the Pharisees of Jesus' day.
- ❑ We don't really need feelings to interfere in our dealings with God.
- ❑ We run the risk of considering only outward behavior and neglecting our inner motives.

What happens if we emphasize emotions and neglect intellect?

____

____

Inwardness that produces true spiritual vitality is dependent on both the heart and the mind. No wonder Jesus asks us to love the Lord God with all our hearts, souls, minds, and strength (Mark 12:30). And Paul encouraged the Philippians to let the mind of Christ indwell their own (Phil. 2:5, KJV). Such invitations never champion a division between the heart and the brain. Thought and emotion are both essential for meditation on the law of God—a law that reveals God's holiness and baptizes us in delight.

I'm glad you're with me in this study. The joys of the table in the wilderness call to every follower of Jesus. In the words of Hebrews, "let us then go to Him outside the camp" (13:13). This time, however, He calls us to meet Him for fellowship rather than disgrace.

End your day's study by writing Christ a letter expressing your feelings for Him.

Now be still before Him and just listen. Write down any thoughts He impresses on your heart.

Day 3 GUARDING THE QUIET PLACES

He is like a tree planted by streams of water, which yields its fruit in season.—Psalm 1:3

In true inwardness God declares Himself without the hard sell. Inwardness is the automatic result of planting ourselves by the continually refreshing streams of God. Evangelism is the blaring trumpet that calls the lost to Christ, but bearing fruit happens in silence. Fruit trees are never noisy in producing fruit. Orchards make apples in silence.

I used to wonder why Francis of Assisi or Theresa of Avila or San Juan de la Cruz never gave the world a scheme of witnessing, a so-called plan of salvation. Theresa spoke for God out of her appetite for Him. Her life held the proclamation of inner reality. Francis of Assisi did not lead people to Jesus as modern evangelists do. He hungered to be an instrument of God's peace, and from this hunger was born an affair of heart that awakened his world to the reality of Christ.

In Avila, once, I stood before the narrow, low-ceilinged cell where Theresa and San Juan de la Cruz prayed. In that cell, their inner lives became so vibrant that it is said they levitated, rising against gravity toward the heaven-enthroned Christ they adored. Whether or not they actually rose from the floor is not central. What is important is that they nurtured an inner life so strong it did indeed break those mental tethers that bound them to the world at hand.

The cords of ordinary living are severed in Christ. Dull gravity cannot bind us to this earth, for heaven indwells us. Planted by rich streams of water, our lives produce fruit.

In contrast, when *Jonathan Livingston Seagull* was being filmed, the cameras in some shots focused on gulls in flight. But the gulls were really tied to a perch with strings. They only appeared to be free. Likewise, while giving the appearance of spiritual freedom, many of us are tied to earthly concerns. How thick are the cords that bind us to Christian reputation!

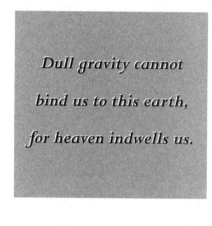

Dull gravity cannot bind us to this earth, for heaven indwells us.

Outward appearance fastens us to our own false needs for approval. I think of how often, as a pastor, I have "acted godly" because people expected me to act that way. Only the journey inward could release me from the strings of my dull religious propriety. On the inward journey I meet Christ, who always delivers me from the bondage of outward expectation.

In your experience, what happens when we "act godly" to try to meet other people's expectations?

____

____

____

____

____

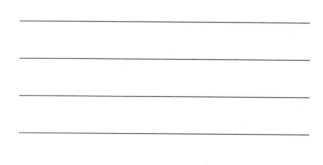

Mark each of the following *true* or *false* according to Galatians 1:10.

____ Paul was concerned with pleasing other people.
____ We cannot please God when seeking the approval of people.
____ Serving God will automatically offend people.

Outwardness and inwardness are the poles of spirituality just as north and south are poles of the earth's geography. Outwardness consists of observable qualities of faith. Outwardness bandages the suffering in the clear sight of all who will behold compassion. It goes to church, lifts the communion wafer, holds a hymnal, bends the knees, and says prayers. It drops coins in offering plates, posts its public pledges, listens, sermonizes, sings, witnesses, and works its way from prison to hospital. Only the second response above was true. Serving God doesn't necessitate offending people, but pleasing them easily takes the place of serving Him.

Outwardness is good but easily spoiled. A few pats on the back can wean it from its love for Christ and draw it toward self-interest. Soon outwardness, which first served the Lord only, finds ways to serve itself while it serves Christ. At last it moves away from the Savior altogether and finds a godlike glory in its own interests. Because it will not be planted by the rivers of God, it becomes root-dried. It withers inwardly while it pretends outwardly that it is well nourished.

Have you experienced your outward service becoming confused with or overcome by self-interest? ❑ yes ❑ no ❑ not sure

If so, identify an example in general terms.

____

Many examples show outwardness gone bad. Outwardness often becomes an unending spiritual performance that lasts until the actor drops from empty exhaustion.

A friend of mine at first found pleasure in his attempts to please his congregation. Later those same desires nearly drove him mad because no matter how hard he tried, nothing he did pleased them. His sermons fell flat. His programs fizzled. His leadership was questioned. Finally his own failures brought him to the edge of insanity, and he resigned his pastorate. Only then did the crushing circumstances of his "failures" drive him to inwardness beyond the outward show. His own inadequacy, at last, brought life to what had been spiritual pretense. When he at last rooted himself in the inward streams of God's depth, he began to bear outward fruit.

Underline key statements in the next two paragraphs describing the religion of the Pharisees.

Christ strongly denounced the dry outwardness of the Pharisees. The word *hypocrite,* which Christ often applied to the Pharisees, refers to an actor's mask. The Pharisees dressed themselves as God's champions while keeping their own visibility a first priority. "They do everything to be observed by others: They enlarge their phylacteries and lengthen their tassels. They love the place of honor at banquets, the front seats in the synagogues, greetings in the marketplaces, and to be called 'Rabbi' by people" (Matt. 23:5-7). The Pharisees really loved their showy spirituality. They knew where to find the nourishing God of the river but chose instead to dwell in the dry deserts of self-importance.

Later in Matthew 23, Jesus pronounced seven woes on the showiness that had degenerated into spiritual narcissism. Listen to Christ's condemnations of their "holy" exhibitionism: "You … make long prayers just for show" (Matt. 23:14). Christ criticized them for evangelism that only brought their converts to the captivity of their own suffocating, spiritual showiness (Matt. 23:15). Their passion for orthodoxy shut God out of the central areas of their faith (Matt. 23:16-22). They kept laws but bypassed compassion (Matt. 23:23). Christ likened them to cups that were clean on the outside but germ-infested on the inside (Matt. 23:25). He said they were mausoleums with beautiful fronts that concealed inner decay (Matt. 23:27). Their outwardness honored traditions but killed the truth (Matt. 23:29-36).

What happened to turn the once-dedicated order of the Pharisees into a synonym for hypocrisy?

____

____

____

____

I do not believe that these Jewish scholars saw themselves as selfish or exhibitionist. They believed they were defenders of Mosaic law and purifiers of national morality. They were ministers of religion and keepers of truth. Their robes marked them as professionals, not phonies. Their phylacteries didn't seem overly large to them, for they contained the holy law and were worn by holy men. Surely, considering what they contained, no phylactery could be too large. In their own minds they weren't trying to follow their own opinions—but the words of their Holy God. Can one ever have too good a reputation? It was right that those they served should respect and revere them. To these, Jesus' words must have sounded unjustifiably critical.

Do you think the same fate that befell the Pharisees could happen to committed disciples in our day? ❑ yes ❑ no ❑ I'm not sure

If so, what might be the warning signs that we are slipping into hypocrisy?

____

____

____

____

____

Hypocrisy cannot define the instant of its birth. It is hard to measure just how much of our worship is for God and how much is for our own reputations. This has been one of my primary concerns as a pastor. I believe our worship is generally offered to Christ, but I often turn to find I have only used His name to sanctify my own. I want to please Christ, and yet I am so easily diverted from His pleasure to mine by the simple phrase: "That was a fine sermon, pastor!" I am suddenly drawn to pursue the compliment rather than the Christ.

For you, how great a temptation is the urge to enhance your own reputation?

a slight problem ——————————— a constant struggle

Let me be clear. Outwardness is as important as inwardness, and either may be phony or real. As inwardness leads to a God addiction, outwardness leads to an ego addiction. We need to remember that the same Jesus who said, "Be careful not to practice your righteousness in front of people, to be seen by them" (Matt. 6:1) also said, "Everyone who acknowledges Me before men, I will also acknowledge him before My Father in heaven" (Matt. 10:32).

Outwardness has for its greatest strength and greatest weakness the same thing: visibility. Likewise, the strength and weakness of inwardness is the same: invisibility. Inwardness draws us to that unseen reality. But it may sin secretly by dividing its own intent, scheming to make life better for both God and the worshiper at once.

We are the keepers of inwardness, and we tend it alone. Our guardianship is utterly crucial, since out of the heart come "the issues of life" (Prov. 4:23, KJV). As someone once pointed out, we are like a ripe fruit that, when squeezed, drips with its real definition.

According to Jesus, being kosher isn't crucial. It's not what goes into our mouths—what we eat or drink—but what comes out of our hearts that defiles us (Matt. 15:11). What comes out shows our inner substance: "As [a man] thinketh in his heart, so is he" (Prov. 23:7, KJV). God focuses his attention on our inwardness. "Man looks at the outward appearance, but the LORD looks at the heart" (1 Sam. 16:7).

As a youth I looked for evidences of God's reality. I wanted Him to speak audibly—even just one word—so I could be sure of His existence. If only He would manifest Himself for a single minute, I would be content, having the concrete evidence of His reality in hand. But my youthful searchings always stopped at the surface of faith until I learned that Christ must be found inside:

In search of God I often take
My ordered world apart
To learn that when my search was done
I found Him at my very heart.[3]

Inwardness is the table where the believer and the Lord meet. I will speak of the heart as the place of rendezvous. In this small meeting place exists the inwardness we consider. It is a wonderful inwardness, nurtured by the stream of life, and ever yielding fruit.

Day 4 THREE WITHERING PARADOXES

He is like a tree planted by streams of water ...

whose leaf does not wither.—Psalm 1:3

Three paradoxes complicate our work and threaten to wither our souls. The first puzzle is the "aloneness is presence" paradox. The second is "retreat is advancement," and the third is "beyond is within."

Aloneness is Presence

In "Prayer...The Priority!" Jack Taylor wrote, "No individual's prayer life will be greater than the quality of his regular time set aside to meet God alone."[4] We must establish inner silence, or we cannot hear the indwelling Christ with whom we desire to speak. I will deal with this silence in a later chapter, but for now I must say that it is established by certain premeditative disciplines that clear away the debris and the noise of life.

Inner silence is easiest to achieve in a place of outer silence. Jesus spoke of the prayer closet in Matthew 6:6 (KJV). In this closet we shut out as much human noise as possible. Yet we are not to covet the silence. We are never to pursue inwardness; We are to pursue Christ. Quietness makes the pursuit effective.

Meditative systems that clear the heart but cannot refill it with substance have no power. In Eastern religions, many devotees of yoga cleanse their minds but leave them empty. Soon their minds refill with the same sort of congestion they had just swept away.

Of what additional danger did Christ warn in Matthew 12:43-45?

____

____

____

Inwardness seeks someone to preside over the clean and the quiet. When Christ comes in, we have provided ourselves an inner worship that is proper. We are not alone in this quietness; we are with Him. Inwardness is a reigning presence and a quiet friend—a person, not a concept. The paradox is set: aloneness is the presence.

How great a challenge do you find aloneness to be?

- ❑ I look forward to and long for my times alone with Christ.
- ❑ I find myself bombarded and distracted by the things I need to be doing.
- ❑ I try to quiet my mind, but it seems so difficult.
- ❑ I focus my thoughts on the Lord and He renews my strength.
- ❑ Other response ________________________

____

____

Retreat is Advancement

The second paradox is that retreat is advancement. To some who desire inwardness, time alone with God may not seem to yield anything practical in their personal plans or career. So why spend time with God when so many important things have to be done?

When the British writer Malcolm Muggeridge visited the monastery at Nunraw, Scotland, he expected to find a group of men who had little to do with the society at large. But he discovered that these men prayed fervently for national and international matters. Because their retreat gave them unbroken touch with the One who holds the very universe in His hand, their prayers were capable of affecting the outward world of finance, politics, and social injustice, as well as their inner selves.

Mark the spot on the graph below showing how you tend to regard prayer.

■———————————————————■

extremely practical ... doesn't change the real world

When we speak of praying monks, we formalize prayer by seeing it as a retreat. Prayer must have that dimension, to be sure. But later in our study, we will also consider continual prayer, which does not interrupt our daily life but marches to accompany it. Brother Lawrence said, "The time of business does not differ with me from the time of prayer: and in the noise and clatter of my kitchen, while several persons are at the same time calling for different things, I possess God as if I were upon my knees at the blessed sacrament."[5]

What benefits could come from the constant relationship that Brother Lawrence described?

___

___

___

Still, a retreat of some sort is necessary if we would find God—if we want our time with him to be free of the clatter of life whether in the laundry or office. Brother Lawrence would no doubt confess that his kitchen prayers proceeded from the base he gave them in his more quiet and solitary moments.

Unless we have quiet time set aside to be with God, the other hours committed to our schedules may be ill-used. Some Christians are prone to ignore times of retreat because to them, ministering seems more important; doing seems better than praying. But prayer is doing. Retreat is not idleness; it is a rigorous discipline of the inner self. We must not let even ministry to others supplant it. Mother Teresa of Calcutta said, "Pray for me that I not loosen my grip on the hands of Jesus even under the guise of ministry to the poor."[6]

Put yourself in the place of one of the apostles and read Luke 9:1-6. How do you think you would feel about the things you were doing?

___

___

___

Why do you think Jesus did what He did in Luke 9:10?

___

___

___

Retreat is advancement; prayer, even extended prayer, is a practical way to use our time—especially those of us who are busy. Martin Luther's philosophy was, "I have so many things to do today, I dare not ignore my time with God." Jesus apparently wanted to the disciples to stay balanced between service and alone time.

Beyond is Within

The third paradox is that beyond is within. The heavens do "declare the glory of God" (Ps. 19:1), yet the Christ who strides the galaxies gathers at a quiet communion with our selves. We do not contain all the fullness of God—we are too small for that—but we are possessed by a transgalactic Omnipotence who chooses to fill our smallness with His vastness.

Our problem is this: We often discover Christ first within some denominational or parachurch ghetto. Having met Him in a province, catching some little view, we are content to paint him in smaller strokes. We then reduce the Lion of Judah to something kittenish because our understanding cannot, at first, write larger definitions.

In what ways have you tried to paint Jesus in smaller strokes by making Him fit your own experience?

____

____

In a sense, Jesus' own description of Himself was too great for the Jewish establishment of His day.

- "Before Abraham was, I am," He said (John 8:58, KJV).
- "I am the living bread which came down from heaven" (John 6:51, KJV).
- "Do you think I cannot call on my Father and he will at once put at my disposal more than twelve legions of angels?" He declared triumphantly (Matt. 26:53).
- "Men will see the Son of Man coming in clouds with great power and glory" (Mark 13:26).

Statements like these overfill the ordinary vessels of small hearts.

Day 5 THREATS TO INNER FULLNESS

The wicked ... are like chaff that the wind blows away.... The LORD watches over the way of the righteous, but the way of the wicked will perish.—Psalm 1:4,6

The poet makes it clear that it is no compliment to be "like the chaff that the wind blows away." Chaff is despicable because it is worthless. So when the wind drives it away, who cares? Good riddance.

I grew up working in the wheat fields of the oceanic American plains. Throughout my teen years, I scooped wheat in the harvest fields. I never got over the joy of reaching down and getting a handful of sweet ripe wheat—golden and sun-warmed—and crunching it in my mouth like "Oklahoma pecans." But occasionally I would get a bit of chaff in my mouthful of wheat. How barbed and coarse, how raspy and grating is chaff.

Just as the bitter chaff spoiled the sweet taste of the pure grain, so three dangers that bar our way to inner fullness spoil the joys of inwardness. Today we'll examine these three dangers.

Depth Addiction

First, the desire to go deeper breeds its own addiction and may keep us from seeing the needs of our world. The best ministry to others always originates from a depth of spirit. Any time we pursue the inner Christ with such zeal that we forget to care about the outer world of lostness and human hurt, our hunger of heart becomes a perversion.

Which of the following could themselves become idols that lead us away from a true walk with Christ?

❑ church attendance
❑ Bible study
❑ writing Christian books
❑ a job in ministry
❑ service to the poor
❑ all of the above

Jesus said unless we have ministered to those about us, we have not ministered to Him (Matt. 25:44-45). This issue requires a delicate balance. We must see with bifocal vision the Christ who is within us and the Christ who hides Himself in needy souls. To lose the view of either Christ is to live as a stranger to both God and man. Any of the choices above—and a thousand more—can go from godly service to ways to hide from people and substitutes for a relationship with Christ.

Have you known Christians who have become so spiritually superior in their own eyes that they could not stoop to be involved in the mundane tasks of life? ❑ yes ❑ no ❑ not sure

If so list below the graces they need to be more rounded followers of Christ.

____

____

Take time to pray for blessings in the lives of those believers.

Otherworldliness

A second danger is that people will see our quest as otherworldly. "You are too heavenly minded to be much earthly good," they say.

How would you explain to a new Christian the dual dangers of neglecting the inner life of devotion or neglecting the outward life of corporate worship and service?

____

____

____

The only answer we can give is that we have entered a life that holds stock in the next world as it hungers to redeem the present one. We who adore Christ are not trying to get out of the pain and pressures of life. We are simply taking steps to infuse life with meaning. The present is but the narrow preface to the eternal. Our role is to do all we can to help the world see that if this age is all we own, we will shortly be disinherited.

The "Sweet-Jesus" Syndrome

The third danger is that we shall be trapped in the "sweet-Jesus" syndrome. The hymn writer is right—there is a sweetness in communion with our Lord. How often the word *sweet* appears in our description of our understanding of Jesus: "Sweet little Jesus boy"; "There's a sweet, sweet spirit in this place"; "Swing low, sweet chariot"; "Sweet hour of prayer." This high-calorie addiction often gets so sticky it gums up ordinary worship. But even worse, it addicts us to the lovely feeling we hold for Jesus rather than to Jesus Himself.

How do you distinguish between your own feelings and Jesus Himself?

____

____

____

____

With these cautions in mind, we are now ready to begin. Let us add to the counsel of Psalm 1 the truth at the center of this book: Fellowship with Christ can only be experienced at a wilderness table for two. Inwardness is not a gaudy party but the meeting of ardent lovers in the lonely desert of the human heart. There, where our wide involvements are reduced only to

Christ and ourselves, we bask in a healing togetherness. There, Christ speaks as much as we do, and even when both of us say nothing, we are rapt in a welded oneness. His perfect presence is joined with ours.

Review this first week's study and answer the following:

1. From your study what do you most desire for your walk with Christ?

2. What truth, statement, or principle most stands out to you?

3. Write a prayer asking God to work in your life in response to that desire and insight.

---

[1]William Shakespeare, *Hamlet,* in *The Complete Works of Shakespeare,* 4th ed., ed. David Bevington (New York: Longman, 1997), 1094.

[2]"Into My Heart,"The Broadman Hymnal (Nashville:Broadman Press, 1940), 321.

[3]Calvin Miller, *Poems of Protest and Faith* (Grand Rapids, MI: Baker, 1965).

[4]Jack Taylor, "Prayer...The Priority!" in *Future Church,* comp. Ralph W. Neighbour Jr. (Nashville, TN: Broadman, 1980), 80.

[5]Brother Lawrence, *The Practice of the Presence of God* (Mount Vernon, NY: Peter Pauper, 1963), 25.

[6]Mother Teresa, quoted in *Meditative Prayer* by Richard J. Foster (Downers Grove, IL: InterVarsity Press, 1983), 15–16.

WEEK 2

BARRIERS TO THE INWARD JOURNEY

Day 1 THE JOURNEY INWARD

Create in me a pure heart, O God, and renew a steadfast spirit within me. Do not cast me from your presence or take your Holy Spirit from me.

—Psalm 51:10-11

Only Christ can satisfy the hunger of our hearts. He prepares a rich table before us—a bountiful feast of divine fellowship and communion. When we hunger for Him and truly seek Him, this banquet is ours. The Host is our meal. His table is our altar. There are only two chairs at this table. We hurry not into His presence, so we may delight to sit and sup with the Son of God. We hurry not from His presence, for the spell of His nearness holds us hostage to His love.

I must create a System or be enslav'd by another Man's.
William Blake

When Soul and body feed, one sees
Their differing physiologies.
Firmness of apple, fluted shape
Of celery, or tight-skinned grape
I grind and mangle when I eat,
Then in dark, salt, internal heart,
Annihilate their natures by
The very act that makes them I.
C. S. Lewis

What does "the Host is our meal" mean to you?

____

How nourishing do you find the person of Christ?

- ❑ He's truly all I need.
- ❑ He fills a hunger for me nothing else can touch.
- ❑ He's something of a side dish.
- ❑ I'm not sure how to be nourished by Christ.

The intrigue of the table in Psalm 23 has nourished my life as a pastor. But the metaphor jumbles itself in glory. I, as a shepherd, became the sheep; and God became the shepherd. The flock disappeared. There were only two. Jesus, the true Shepherd, walked alone with me. Our sojourn was uninterrupted in the pleasant fields through the threatening chasm and back again. The glory was not the path we walked but our togetherness.

How does it feel for you to walk away from the crowd and spend time alone with Jesus?

____

____

Of the time you spend consciously seeking to relate to Christ, what percentage is:

____ % outward, involving service to or with other people?

____ % inward, involving yourself and Christ alone?

How are we to approach this table in the wilderness? Exactly as we would any other table—hungry. Our hunger is for Him whom we really can never know fully in a group. Groups cannot experience the one-on-one intimacy the table offers us.

Circle any statements in the next paragraph that describe your soul's response or need.

Do we not feel a certain reluctance to be alone with our Host? After all, He knows everything about us. Do we not feel a need for repentance—a yearning to clean up our act—even as we sit at the table? Do we not desire to weep? Should we not relish the spiritual high we feel in His nearness? Yes, but our emotional feasting is not the reason we come to the table. We do not come to vent our emotion. We have come to be with Him.

His presence draws us most powerfully in His direction. Deep feelings may be our response. We may be awash in laughter and tears. But we meet with Christ because we need Him, not because we long to laugh or to cry.

What reason does Psalm 23:3 give for seeking the divine presence?

❑ healing ❑ strength for the journey
❑ forgiveness ❑ the sake of His Name

We will identify a number of barriers to the inner fullness we need. Popular worship may ease our appetites with giddy or glitzy God-talk that makes us feel religious without providing us any real close time with God. Although God seeks to guide us along paths of righteousness to intimacy with Him, we all are prone to stumbling off the path. A host of lesser appetites allure us and war against our hunger of spirit. These allurements prowl the wilderness like young lions in search of prey. They divert us from the better appetites that God desires for our pilgrimage. They spoil the table. We stuff ourselves with frivolous hors d'oeuvres until we have no room for better food.

Would you say that you have ever experienced "junk-food Christianity"?

❑ yes ❑ no ❑ not sure

What excesses have you encountered in your journey to intimacy with God?

❑ frenzied emotionalism ❑ cold legalism
❑ dead formalism ❑ exhausting self-effort
❑ precise correct belief ❑ rigid tradition

Enemies of the Holy erect barriers to keep us from the table of fellowship with God. These young lions seek to keep us tethered to the common, and the physical, knowing that we can't soar with Christ when our feet are in the mud.

Answer the following *true* or *false* based on Paul's words in Romans 7:14-24

___ Paul saw himself as having arrived at perfection.
___ Human nature is basically good.
___ The law makes us aware of our utter sinfulness.
___ A war rages between our mind and our flesh.

The apostle Paul reckoned with the old nature. He hungered for that perfect life that ended in union with Christ, where he would finally set himself free of every lower definition. He cried that no matter how ideal his Christianity became, he was still shackled. He was unable to enjoy an uninterrupted, face-to-face relationship with Christ. He found himself dealing, sometimes unsuccessfully, with fierce yet ordinary drives. His strong desire to please the Savior became snarled in demanding contradictions: "I discover this principle: when I want to do good, evil is with me" (Rom. 7:21). The answers were false, false, true, true.

Does knowing the apostle Paul also struggled
❑ encourage or ❑ discourage you? Why?

___

___

___

The inner struggle is titanic, but we can learn valuable lessons. For one thing, this same continuous quarrel rages in every Christian. Our most determined efforts at personal reform do not last long. Our poor resolve crushes them like New Year's resolutions. We cannot win with mere willpower. We win only as we achieve a constant walk with Christ. Our effort has too little fiber in its intention. Our discipline is a matter of the inner reign of Christ. He will be victorious when we give him His full sovereignty over our weak intentions.

How does "giving Christ His full sovereignty over our weak intentions" differ from "our efforts at personal reform"?

____

____

____

____

Even Christ himself did not escape the battle. "The Word became flesh and took up residence among us" (John 1:14). He understood what it meant to be human in every respect. In becoming a man, Christ shattered mere humanness as a barrier to inwardness. Christ proved that spiritual life can both indwell and empower the natural life. We are more than thinking, praying, digestive tracts. We are worshiping persons. We need not succumb to the attack of the roaring young lions. With discipline and God's help, we can overcome these snarling beasts that bar the way to our inner fellowship with him.

This week we will examine some of these barriers to inwardness that we must guard against if we are to enjoy communion with the Holy.

Day 2 EMPTINESS, SHALLOWNESS, AND SIN

[The Lord] satisfies the thirsty and fills the hungry with good things.—Psalm 107:9

God intended us to have an energizing relationship with Him at the center of our being. Instead we tend to substitute emptiness, shallowness, and sin. Today we'll look at the first three barriers to inwardness.

Barrier One: Emptiness

We are vessels. God created us to be receptacles of Himself, but in spite of the Holy Spirit's readiness to invade our lives, most of us hold nothing. Our inner lives—created by God to contain Himself—hold only little trinkets—the tinsel of our egos.

Many years ago, someone gave me an antique wooden dynamite box made in the nineteenth century. For years I prized that box. It was meticulously constructed with mitered corners and bore an ominous warning printed in bold red and black letters: "Danger: Dynamite!" At one time the box had indeed been dangerous; its contents had to be handled gently. But the last time I saw it, the box was filled with common paraphernalia that could be found in any workroom. The box should have read: "Danger: Junk—bits of twine, a half-wound roll of tape, a crooked screwdriver." There's some force in this universe that doesn't like empty boxes! Why? Boxes are vacuums—depressurized spaces that long to draw whatever substance they can into the void. Our emptiness is an abscess. When it is not filled by careful design, it becomes a catchall for secular trivia.

Mark the following *true* or *false* based on what you just read.

___ God intended us to be temples that He would fill.
___ We naturally drift and fill our lives with worthless materials.
___ We can both spend our lives on trivia and grow in Christ.
___ Our lives will be filled one way or another.
___ Our egos co-exist well with Christ's lordship.

My old dynamite box represents a parable of Christians' spirituality. The human spirit is either a treasure chest or a junk box. We were designed to bear the power of God, but the debaucheries of our hearts can quickly fill the space intended for God. Many a saint-in-intention winds up at last only a junk receptacle haphazardly filled with the trivia of superficiality. By the way, I responded T, T, F, T and F to the exercise above.

What would an observer of the typical week of your life conclude that you contain?

____

____

____

Louis Evely, in *That Man Is You,* says even the most derelict of souls contain a hunger for inwardness because we are created in God's image:

> *There's something sonly in each human being;*
> *but how well he hides it,*
> *and how unskillful we are at finding it!*[1]

This "something sonly" is the vacuum of our hearts—a yearning emptiness that strains to be filled with Christ.

Barrier Two: Shallowness

Deep calls to deep in the roar of your waterfalls; all your waves and breakers have swept over me. By day the Lord *directs his love, at night his song is with me.*

—Psalm 42:7-8

Our worship, as well as the content of popular books and sermons, betrays a lack of depth. For so many, popular Christianity seems to be merely the fastest way to personal gain.

Like the writer of Psalm 51, we need to confess that we claim to honor Christ while we worship Narcissus. Ego, not Christ, is the god of the secular Christian. Our slick religious tabloids abound with articles like, "God Saved My Business!" Books (and CDs and videotapes) on Christian aerobics, Christian cosmetics, and Christian diets abound. The medicine-show Christ of the Excedrin consumer always preaches a gospel of prosperity.

What would you say to a friend who said he or she believes God always wants us to be healthy, wealthy, and trouble-free?

____

____

____

____

Some time ago a book entitled, *I Prayed Myself Slim!* told the story of a willowy Cinderella who had been trapped in her own obese body. In a fit of spirituality, she took her overweight condition to Christ. According to her, Jesus helped her lose weight. She was at last transformed into the beautiful princess God intended her to be. She had dates, dates, dates. She was desired by the most exciting bachelors in town. God had rescued her from her fate as a waddling wallflower and cast her into the fast lane of life. Naturally, she gave all the credit to God.

Perhaps our slim young lady should have asked, "Does God want the credit?" The issue is not whether God can help us to be our best selves but whether God's main agenda is to create Cinderellas. In fact, God wants us to glorify His Son, a result of which is to escape the prison of self. Yet a new Christian egotism insists that a "Christianized" self is an adequate center for life.

Only Christ is an adequate center for life. To find this center, we must not look outward, but inward. Spiritual inwardness is a longing to be filled with Christ—the original contents for which God created our "box."

Barrier Three: Sin

Have mercy on me, O God, according to your unfailing love; according to your great compassion blot out my transgressions. Wash away all my iniquity and cleanse me from my sin. Psalm 51:1-2

King David wrote Psalm 51 after the prophet Nathan confronted him about his adulterous affair with Bathsheba. The psalm is a plea for deliverance from basic human appetites that threaten to shut down our communication with God.

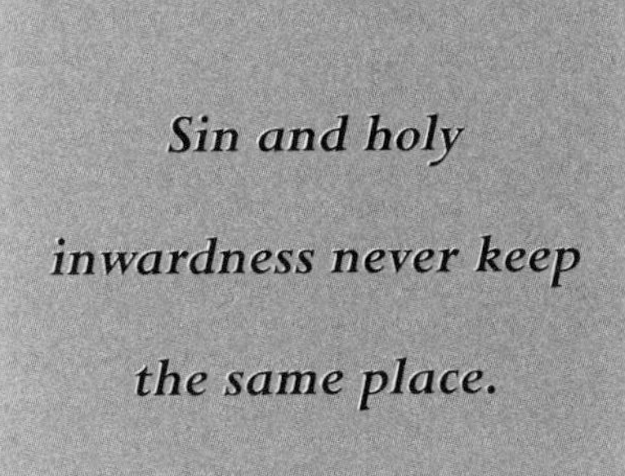
Sin and holy inwardness never keep the same place.

David, in the crisis brought about by his infant son's death and the sting of a prophet's rebuke, comes before God filled with degradation. Adulteries, lies, and murder crowd the center of his soul like a nest of breeding serpents. Each lie breeds another, creating ever more vermin. The poet of God has clearly lost his song and is only an empty shell of rationalized sin.

Let's not rebuke the king too readily. Even in our lives, sin and holy inwardness never keep the same place.

The psalmist must have felt the same struggle with the old nature that Paul would describe centuries later. David is in agony, for he knows the high cost of sin. When sin has run its course, it always divides a believer from God. Therefore he begs: "Blot out, wash away, cleanse!" How welcome is his cry to God. How God thrills each time one of His prodigal children leaves the pigpens of self-indulgence and seeks His presence with David's three-fold petition—"Blot, wash, cleanse!"

How does the thought of losing intimacy with God strike you?

❑ It scares me to death.
❑ I've never had that much intimacy anyway.
❑ I don't think I could lose touch with God.
❑ I have never thought about it.
❑ I long for real intimacy with Him.
❑ Other response ____________________

The thought of losing his intimacy with God terrifies David. "Do not cast me from your presence or take your Holy Spirit from me" (Ps. 51:11). He begs God to blot out his iniquity—to wash away his sin. Why? Because he understands that his sin is a barrier to holiness. God will not restore his lost spiritual intimacy until his heart is pure. The poet knows that one confession will not be adequate to cover all his future struggles with sin. Inner purity is a lifelong struggle.

Our battle with sin is daily. It ever rages against the intimacy of the table. We are all forever in flight from a host of appetites that war against our hunger of spirit. These appetites are driven by the demons of excess. Excess is little more than a legitimate need carried too far. Food is a daily need, and God will gladly supply it. But gluttony is a feast prepared by the tempter. Sex is a gift of God; rape is an orgy of defiance born of hell. Our most terrible excesses are at first birthed in legitimate appetites. These legitimate drives are basic to our need, yet they threaten us as "righteousness gone out of control."

In the following paragraphs underline clues to answer the question: "Why doesn't legalism solve the problem of sin?"

For generations much of the Christian church has foolishly sought to control sin and arrive at holiness by code. To develop these codes we build rigid ethical frameworks. They are but cold and harsh legalisms. In the end, they produce only frustrated disciples. These "spiritual" rules are paper defenses. The trouble is that our rules and codes are never complete. The church covenant of the denomination to which I belong contains prohibitions against the sale and use of alcoholic beverages, but it never mentions the more contemporary evils of drug abuse or racial discrimination. Such legalistic codes also usually say nothing about the less visible, inward sins of jealousy or hatred that destroy our fellowship with the Holy.

Not only are such rules beside the point, but they also set Christians in judgment over each other. A friend of mine once attended a church potluck dinner. She was standing in line behind a man who was smoking a cigarette. "Where do you propose to snuff your tobacco in heaven?" she asked him. The smoker replied, "In your coffee cup." Without rules, such judgments would never pass between believers.

Legalism aborts relationships with both God and others. Its focus is negative. The evil we seek to prohibit grows with concentration into targets we cannot miss. Rules, instead of limiting our sin, define sin—and by defining it rivet our attention to it—and at last lead us to desire it. Great worship, on the other hand, avoids focusing on sin and instead points our hearts and minds in a totally different direction.

What reasons did you find for the failure of legalism to create genuine holiness?

____

____

____

____

____

The best way to deal with sin has never been to attempt reform but to adore the Savior.

The answer to winning over sin is learning to worship. Psalm 51 is more than a wayward king saying, "I'm sorry." It's a snapshot of a broken man falling in love with God all over again. The gall of David's disappointment with himself is mingled with the tears of a restored adoration.

The best way to deal with sin has never been to attempt reform but to adore the Savior. We win over our lower nature through adoration. While we worship the enthroned, inner Christ, we cannot be intrigued or controlled by our negative preoccupations with sin. Legalism fails because: (1) Laws are never complete. (2) They are outward rather than inward. (3) They divide believers with human judging, and (4) they enforce a focus on evil rather than on Christ.

Day 3 SEX AND GLUTTONY

Surely I was sinful at birth, sinful from the time my mother conceived me. Surely you desire truth in the inner parts; you teach me wisdom in the inmost place.—Psalm 51:5-6

David seems to be acknowledging that he had been conceived out of his parents' sexual appetite. Yet in his own life this appetite went awry and cost him dearly. Sexuality and gluttony are two of the seven deadly sins that often travel in pairs.

What does 2 Samuel 5:13 tell you about David?

____

____

How did sexual indulgence affect David's son Solomon according to 1 Kings 11:1-3?

____

____

____

Sexual desire is demanding and constant. It has influenced the history of the world. Initially, the church fathers were extremely zealous in their devotion to God. Some of them began practicing celibacy as a by-product of their commitment. In time, however, the nobility of their self-sacrifice became flawed. In some cases, celibacy became a legalism. Extreme examples occurred. Origen had himself castrated as a literal fulfillment of Matthew 19:12.

What is the difference between sacrificing for Christ and adhering to legalistic rules?

____

____

____

Devotion to Christ is far better when it precedes the rule. Francis of Assisi, for example, proclaimed that he had taken a bride more beautiful than any offering of human companionship. That relationship to Christ led him to live a life of celibacy. His celibacy was not a flaw; it was his gift to God. Francis was not following a rule but pursuing a Lover.

How does your devotion to Christ either help or hinder you in managing your sexual temptations?

____

____

Liberated Christians in our day have taken the subject to press and made sex a more open issue. In a single century, observed Stuart Barton Babbage, we have gone from a culture which talked openly of death and guardedly of sex to one which speaks guardedly about death and openly about sex.

This new open sexuality has become the preoccupation of the arts. The golden gods of lust have become the idolatry of the West. A bumper sticker laments our cultural guilt: "Remember when air was clean and sex was dirty?"

The passion of the glands can serve as a symbol of spiritual love that hungers after God. Human desire can either distract us from spiritual pursuits or point us to our need for Christ. Elizabeth of Hungary, a thirteenth-century mystic, married a lusty crusader named Louis. Elizabeth's passion for Louis drove her to constant lust for him. Merely seeing Louis in church quickened her erotic desire.

But this fierce yearning for Louis was only one aspect of a double madness. Elizabeth also was passionate in her pursuit of the Holy God whom she desired with an equal ardor. She cried out to know the approval of Christ, striving for His pleasure as well.

Food and sex have become the "double jeopardy" of our affluent Western culture.

Mark the following either *true* or *false* concerning human sexual desire and love for Christ.

____ Both are meant to be fulfilling.
____ Both were created and intended by God.
____ Both bring ultimate fulfillment.
____ God intended human love to be a picture of Christ's love.

Fortunately for Elizabeth, she and Louis married. But Louis left their young marriage, feeling a spiritual obligation to go on a crusade. In his continued absence, Elizabeth found the inner and powerful presence of Christ began to motivate her in an equal but higher passion. She ministered through the villages and hostels of the city, giving her life in unending ministry where she took little thought of her own health or the common necessities of life. She died at twenty-four years of age, having served two loves in fullest passion.

Louis and Elizabeth demonstrate that more than a casual connection ties human love and the love of God. This human love we refer to as *eros*. The divine love we call *agape*. Eros is sexual love. Agape is grace love, undeserved love, unconditional love. Did David understand this? Did he know that both kinds of love are motivated by passions not easily denied?

How foolish we are to believe that those who have a great adoration for Christ cease to be sexual creatures. It is tragic that we do not channel our passions and make them usable to God.

But let us turn from the whole issue of sex and focus on another kind of need that is just as easily and frequently perverted. Gluttony lays another snare before the inner life. Gluttony and a rapacious spirit can be alike, if only because both of them can overfeed. Food and sex have become the "double jeopardy" of our affluent Western culture. Restaurateurs and obscenity peddlers continue to keep people occupied with sweetmeats and pornography. Gluttony and libertinism seem to have become accepted ways of life. Francis of Assisi felt that his flesh constantly pressed his ego to indulge at the cost of everything he held proper.

Why do you suppose sex and food so easily lead to excess?

____

____

____

In the church this dichotomy is blatant. At a recent spiritual life conference I attended, the food brought by the parishioners seemed more central than the spiritual food which the visiting pastor offered from the lectern. At such moments, the word *hunger* becomes so gastric we might forget that the church exists to feed the soul.

Gandhi once remarked that those in the abundance of the West were guilty of overfilling themselves. They ate food they did not need because they had lost control of their appetites. No one, he reasoned, would overfill a car with gas; and yet Westerners constantly overfeed themselves.

Hunger is a God-given drive for sustaining life. But gluttony moves ahead of need and eats merely to feel good. Gluttony is a glaring indication of the lack of yieldedness within the Christian community. In banquets and dinners across the nation, we participate in orgies of indulgence. Consider the irony of churches holding conferences to preach the crucified life while they fill their bodies with endless lunches, dinners, and brunches.

Concern about overindulgence has led many Christians to examine anew Christ's command of self-denial. They are looking for sensible responses to the problem of overindulging in food.

What is the difference between fasting as a spiritual discipline and fasting as a religious legalism?

____

____

____

____

The Bible encourages fasting. The discipline has been a part of the church throughout the ages. For Catholics fasting used to be normative before worship. The very word *breakfast* suggests the idea of breaking a fast only after one had drawn close to Christ in the Eucharist. Protestants followed suit. John Wesley refused to ordain anyone into the Methodist ministry who did not commonly fast. Richard Foster wisely calls us to fast and thus to take a stand against all those appetites our indulgence would appease. Fasting bears a great witness to the control of our passions. Gluttony admits we are in bondage to them.

Do you practice fasting? ❑ yes ❑ no
What might be the benefits and liabilities?

____

____

____

What other forms of "overfeeding ourselves" do you think hinder our witness for Christ?

____

____

What other forms of fasting, such as from television might you consider?

____

____

Would you consider setting aside a period of time this week to fast in some form?
❑ yes ❑ no
If so, from what will you fast?

____

Specifically how will you use that time to draw hear to God?

____

____

Day 4 FACING OUR TRANSGRESSION, NAMING OUR SIN

I know my transgressions, and my sin is always

before me.—Psalm 51:3

So often we come to the table of Psalm 23 filled with the unconfessed sins of Psalm 51. But Psalm 51 marks the path back to Psalm 23. True repentance always precedes forgiveness and restored fellowship. Naming our sin is a must for forgiveness to occur.

We don't have to say it aloud (David doesn't actually spell out his sin in this passage), but we have to hold it out in the center of our hearts. We must come clean before God.

David can honestly say, "My sin is ever before me." What he means by this is that his sin is so much before him that it has become a barrier between himself and God. It is a wall of estrangement between him and his loving father.

To you does a wall of estrangement with God feel more like…

- ❑ an aching void
- ❑ something missing
- ❑ quiet desperation
- ❑ quiet desperation
- ❑ an inner stain
- ❑ a deep hunger
- ❑ other__________________________________

David's sin strangled the intimacy he had felt with God when he wrote the Twenty-third Psalm. Oh, the difference between the two men who wrote these two psalms! Yet they are the same person. The difference is that Psalm 23 was written by a David who treasured holiness and an intimate relationship with God. Psalm 51 was written by a David who had committed adultery and murder.

Now the earlier David has been devoured by the ravenous caprice of the later David. Further, he knows only one way back—repentance. He must set his sin in front of God. He must confess it.

Have you in some sense devoured an earlier, more idealistic version of yourself?
❑ yes ❑ no ❑ I'm not sure

What kinds of pressures urge us to abandon our ideals as we go through life?

____

____

____

Does God not know David has sinned? If God knows David has sinned, and David does too, why does David need to repent? Repentance is not informing God of our waywardness; it is our agreement to stand with God and look on it together. As we both study it, we agree that it is sin.

Forgiveness does not consist of cluing God in on our sin life. Being forgiven is taking 1 John 1:9 at its word: "If we confess our sins, He is faithful and righteous to forgive us our sins and to cleanse us from all unrighteousness." It is confessing—agreeing with God—that we have sinned so he can forgive us. The Greek word here translated "confess" is *homologeō*—to agree with God that we have done wrong.

Repentance is our willingness to stand with God and look at our sin. While we stand together and stare at it, God says, "Cast down your eyes from that noble altar of Christ's cross. I sent my Son to die for you. Can you live no better than this?"

Against God Only

Against you, you only, have I sinned and done what is evil in your sight, so that you are proved right when you speak and justified when you judge.—Psalm 51:4

Notice the catalog of David's sins. David's spirit of self-sacrifice had eroded into self-indulgence. His "take-it-easy" attitude had led him to stay home when his army was in the field (2 Sam. 11:1). He had traded self-denial for comfort. Then came the gradual degradation of his willfully sinning soul. His lust for another man's wife led him into adultery (2 Sam. 11:4). His lust for ego approval led him next to commit murder (2 Sam. 11:15-17). But mercifully, at last, he wound his way downward to the altar of his brokenness. There David learned that we were intended to be more than the sum of our drives.

David had wronged a great host of people by his adulterous, murderous sins. Still, until he comes to see that his real sin is against God, he has little hope of being forgiven.

Our new cultural postmodern credo for avoiding sin is, "Hurt no one and do what you please." I've seen such bumper stickers in many university parking lots. It's true that if no one hurt anybody with self-centered living, this would be a better world; but it might still be self-centered. I much prefer Augustine's credo for avoiding sin: "Love God and do what you please."

The real truth is that, if we love God, we will only do what pleases God. My suspicion is that a secular hedonist who hurts no one may still have chosen a life that is too self-indulgent to be of much value in a hurting world.

Sin hurts God by damaging the world as He would like it to be. But sin hurts us by driving a wedge between ourselves and our holy God, who wants His children to live in close relationship with Him.

Confession brings the totality of our sin to God and admits that it is "only God" we have wronged. But is this true? Against God only? Can this be David's plea? Did he not wrong the nation? Did he not take advantage of Bathsheba? Did he not wrong Uriah in arranging for his murder? How then can he say, "against God only"? "Only" must be understood in this context as "first" and "primarily."

On the basis of what you just read, answer the following *true* or *false*.

____ 1. Sin is exclusively against God.

____ 2. We can do what we please as long as we don't hurt anybody.

____ 3. Putting God first has a way of correcting all our other behaviors.

____ 4. Sin hurts God but also hurts ourselves and others.

____ 5. David wronged many people, but his sin was primarily against God.

____ 6. Forgiveness depends on our getting to our root sin—against God.

David hurt God primarily. The mess he made of so many lives would have been solved if he had loved God only. It was when he quit loving God first that he became a moral liability in God's world. The first two statements are false. The rest are true.

Barrier Number Four: Power Drive

Cleanse me with hyssop, and I will be clean: wash me, and I will be whiter than snow. Let me hear joy and gladness; let the bones you have crushed rejoice. Hide your face from my sins and blot out all my iniquity.—Psalm 51:7-9

Power forms the fourth barrier to inwardness. In Psalm 51, David is confessing that his vaulting ambition had caused him to feel he had the right to take what he wanted from life. What was the real sin from which he wanted God to hide his face? Was it not the sin of unbridled power?

Power leads those who cherish it to feel they can take anything they please, because they see themselves as in a special moral category of entitlement. I am entitled! I can take what I want, when I want it. I don't have to answer to anyone—even to God. So all of David's sins might be lumped under the presumption of power. The lust for power lures those who desire it to make it a towering god above all smaller gods.

Have you ever been tempted to feel a sense of entitlement? ❑ yes ❑ no
If so, what was the temptation?

____

____

David certainly was aware that his lust for power had become a barrier to inwardness. Careers, even religious careers, may become little more than forums for our own advancement. How are we to deal with such ambition? Our longing after Christ must exceed our need for status in the world.

The drive for power is common to all. We want to control as vast a domain as possible. Did not the tempter entice Adam and Eve with the prospect of being like gods? Satan inflamed them with a lust for power. Satan told Eve she could rise from humanity to godhood in one simple act. Satan's offer of personal power will always be stated as not just benefiting us but also being of use to God and others. We all like to think of ourselves as generous and self-giving. We all like to hear others tell us how humble or spiritual we are. Such comments rarely draw us closer to Christ. In fact, they most often separate us from God. Compliments are the parents of egotism, and egotism seldom stops celebrating its own power long enough to marvel at God's.

Egotism seldom stops celebrating its own power long enough to marvel at God's.

If "compliments are the parents of egotism," should we compliment others? Why or why not?

____

____

How does complimenting someone differ from encouragement or affirmation?

____

____

How can we affirm our children without making egotists of them?

____

____

David, like many powerful people, had begun to enjoy and abuse his own smug sense of entitlement. No doubt at the moment of his fall he may have told himself, "I shall do what I will. I am, after all, a king!" Power often congratulates itself by dropping the same moral requirements it forces on other people. (see 2 Sam. 12:5-6)

David then passed by the obligation of remembering that only God is great. Power, born in church politics and burdensome hierarchies, can also separate us from our Host. The poet James Kavanaugh said he was not able to find God at all while he held the power and position of a priest. For him, God was born in his very renunciation of his priesthood.

How have you seen power congratulate itself "by dropping the same moral requirements it forces on other people"?

- ❑ parents telling their children: "do as I say, not as I do"
- ❑ politicians who disobey the law
- ❑ Christians who don't "practice what they preach"
- ❑ people in business abusing the power of their position
- ❑ the temptation to take shortcuts "because I can"
- ❑ other______________________________

____

May the psalmist be our teacher. We cannot grasp for personal power and attain meaningful fellowship with God at the same time. Yet this is the heart of religious positivism in America. We belittle Christ by trying to advance both our causes and His at once. Incredibly, Adam and Eve were led to believe they were actually becoming like God by serving their own interests. When they fled and hid from God the Almighty with their half-eaten fruit, they were ashamed at thinking they were capable of being like God. Their knowledge of good and evil was not a strength.

How great a temptation do you find "trying to advance both your cause and Christ's at once"?

a gentle tug ■——————■ a giant pull

Religious hucksters still stay too near the tree of good and evil. They advertise their fruit with the promise that our best interest also advances the cause of God. "Make God your copilot," they cry, forgetting that God has his own plans for the destiny of each one of us.

In another time, Theresa of Avila knew that the Host would not join her at the wilderness table if her life was marked by ambition. She begged, in her introduction to *Way of Perfection,* for the church to strip everything from her writing that might embarrass Christ. She pleaded her editor to change or burn her work should it prove only a testament to her ambition.

We too must stand against Adam's ambition. We must shun the temptation to become as gods. To linger when we are complimented, to make too much of personal affirmations, to study our own cleverness—all of these can addict us to human praise and steal from us our desire to have more of Christ.

Day 5 BARRIER FIVE: HURRIEDNESS

Create in me a pure heart, O God, and renew a steadfast spirit within me. . . . The sacrifices of God are a broken spirit; a broken and contrite heart, O God, you will not despise.—Psalm 51:10,17

Our last barrier to full intimacy with the Savior is hurriedness. Intimacy may not be rushed. To meet with the Son of God takes time. We have learned all too well the witless art of living fast. We gulp our meals sandwiched in between pressing obligations. The table of communion with the inner Christ is not a fast-food franchise. We cannot dash into His presence and choke down inwardness before we hurry on to our one o'clock appointment. Inwardness is time-consuming, open only to minds willing to sample spirituality in small bites, savoring each one. It is difficult to teach the unhurried discipline of the table to a culture brought up on frozen dinners and condensed novels.

How difficult do you find it to stop and quiet your mind?

❑ I can do it only with serious effort.
❑ It's easy for me.
❑ Can I get back to you on that?

Inwardness does not rest comfortably with hyped-up revivalism. It is off limits to those who are in a rush to get to know God. The intense appeals of fast-lane religion are so outward that they miss the heart. Tears and hysteria get in the way of godly conversation. Fierce emotionalism blinds us to the delights of the table.

Intimacy with Christ comes from entering His presence with inner peace rather than bursting into His presence from the hassles of life. T. S. Eliot well described our dilemma when he wrote, "Where shall the world be found, where will the word resound? Not here, there is not enough silence." The church fathers spoke of *otium sanctum,* or "holy leisure."[2] A relaxed contemplation of the indwelling Christ allows for an inner communion impossible to achieve while oppressed by busyness and care.

But David's travail of soul came because of his unholy leisure. Then a willful king, who thought not to go to war, would take a little time off. But these undisciplined hours were not his friends. Unholy leisure is free time that results in wasted living. Unholy leisure is to have undisciplined time on our hands. When we do not make the clock serve a noble purpose, it becomes a sluggish timepiece giving us only the curse of excess.

Perhaps you are wondering how I harmonize what I have said in other places about goal setting and discipline with this imperative for leisure. They are not as contradictory as they appear. When we learn to manage time, we are not managed by time. Once we become masters of our schedule, we will actually create the "extra" time we need to approach God in peace.

Those who have not learned this come to God as they do everything else—late! They rush into the presence of the great white throne, a tornado of hurriedness. They blurt out their confessions and whisk on to the next appointment, glad that they have managed to work God into their blustery schedules.

Otium sanctum is true leisure set squarely down in the middle of a busy life. Most of our hurriedness is really a cover for sloth. When we cram our calendars with appointments, we may delude ourselves that we are busy. But busy about what? We are tending the whirligigs of the trivial—afraid that if we stop, we might actually come face to face with the emptiness of our lives.

We can hardly enjoy the table in the wilderness if we are always looking at our watches, wondering how much time we may reasonably give our Host. Holy living is not abrupt living. No one who hurries into the presence of God is content to remain for long. Those who hurry in, hurry out. Holy leisure prepares us to receive the gift of inwardness.

What "whirligigs of the trivial" scream for pieces of your time?

____

____

How do you think your life would be different if you could truly practice *otium sanctum?*

____

____

The psalmist wisely reckoned that the sacrifices of God are a broken spirit. The heart is mended by years of intimate resting in God and not with the hasty prayers and hurried bargains of our "good deals for God."

For many years now I have practiced what I call "kenotic meditation." The idea first occurred to me in reading Philippians 2:5-8, which states that Jesus emptied

Himself of the glory of God and took on humanity. The word *kenotic* comes from the Greek word meaning "to empty." As Jesus once emptied Himself of divine honor to please His Father, so I must empty myself of the hurriedness of life to please Christ.

Before I really begin to talk to God, I like to take a quarter of an hour to shut my mind against the busyness of the world. Incessant chatter fills our thoughts and keeps our brains swimming in images. We must not only stop obscene or irrelevant thinking, we must deal with the froth and spin of unceasing mental images. This is not easy, but as I move closer to this imageless state of being, my mind slows down to a cleansed level of quietness. At this point, I am able to receive the Host with undivided attention.

During my childhood, our house in rural Oklahoma had little furniture on its plain, plank flooring. But if ever we expected company, my mother transformed that little house into a room of grand hospitality. Every visitor was welcomed by a thoroughly clean, neat house. Jesus needs to be shown this same respect.

David's cry for a clean heart is really a cry for a quiet heart. Lead me "beside quiet waters," he pleads. Restore my soul! (see Ps. 23:2-3) The noise of his sin had drowned out the safer symphonies of his lost obedience.

The emptying of the mind can be achieved with any posture so long as it is in absolute solitude. It is best to close your eyes to eliminate visual distractions. Once your eyes are closed, you simply rest the mind, forcing every thought into silence as it arises. Some have confessed to me that they think immediately of God as soon as they begin the emptying process. But I feel this is unwise. God becomes too quickly wed to images we are trying to clear away. Others have felt that to empty the mind without filling it immediately with Christ will make way for demons to capture our souls. We would be better off to fear the demons of busyness and self-importance that already have charge of our frenzied souls. But the real point is this: The cleansed heart is the only proper place where Christ may enter us and live.

Set aside a time to quiet your mind and prepare your heart for a visit with the King. If you cannot make the time right now, in the margin write the time you will spend at least 15 minutes in silence with the Lord.

The Intimacy of Worship

O Lord, open my lips, and my mouth will declare

your praise. Psalm 51:15

True worship craves intimacy, and intimacy is only achieved as we come to Him crying out the Fifty-first Psalm: cleanse, blot, wash.

The young lions of emptiness, shallowness, sexuality, gluttony, power, and hurry roar against our desire to be conformed to Christ's image. Our appetites order us away from the pleasure of our Host. Only as we steel ourselves against overfilling these hungers will the table be unspoiled. But when we take charge, we will sit alone with Christ, ever longing for the life we find in Him alone. And when finally the time comes, our Host will sense our love and know that our hunger for Him will bring us back to the table again and again. In His enduring presence, we utter, "Surely goodness and mercy shall follow me all the days of my life" (Ps. 23:6 KJV).

---

[1]Louis Evely, *That Man Is You,* trans. Edmond Bonin (New York; Paulist, 1963), 107.

[2]T. S. Eliot, "Ash-Wednesday," in *The Waste Land and Other Poems* (New York: Harcourt Brace Jovanovich, 1962), 64.

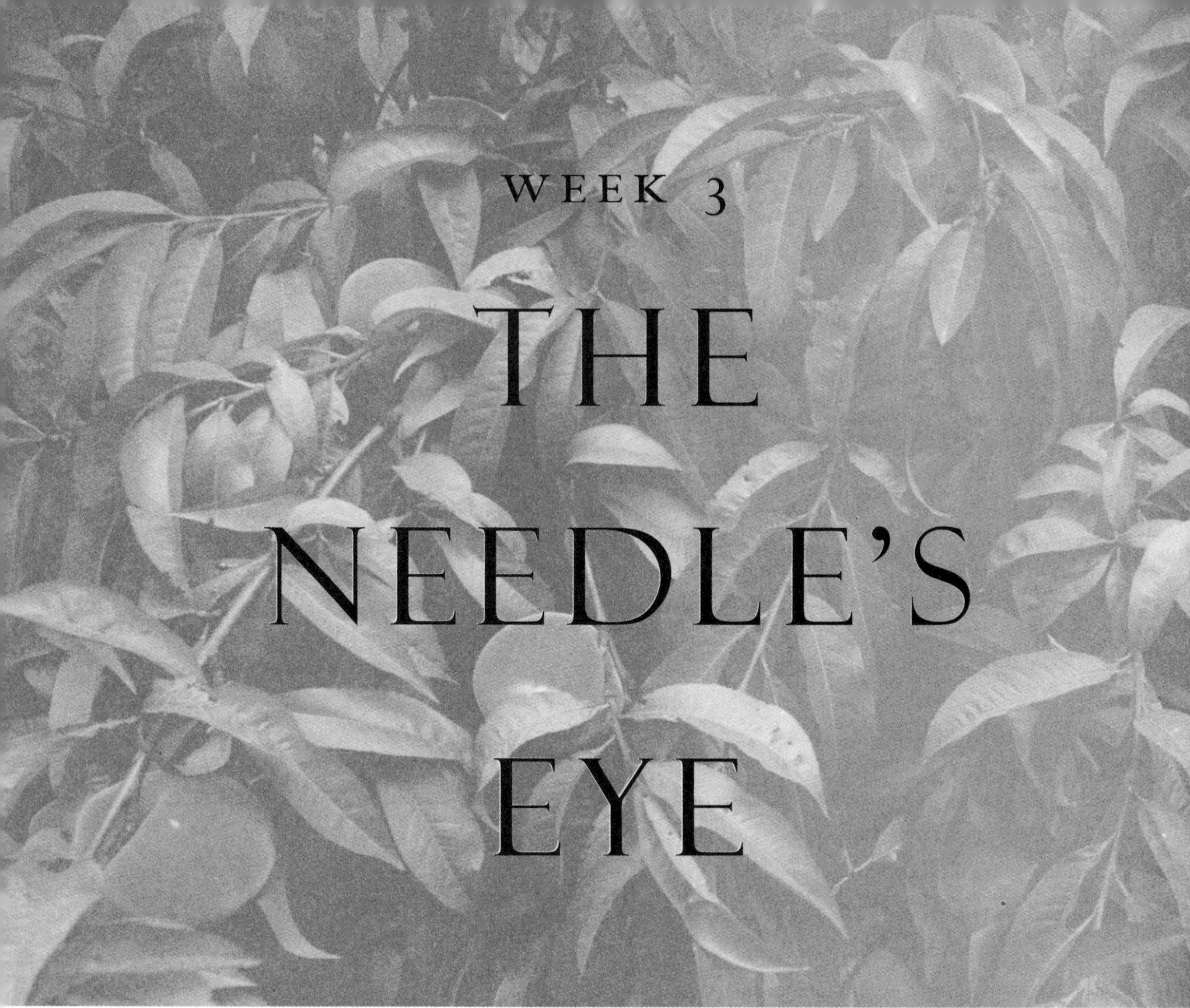

WEEK 3

THE NEEDLE'S EYE

Day 1 A MISPLACED ADMIRATION

Do not fret because of evil men or be envious of those who do wrong; for like the grass they will soon wither, like green plants they will soon die away.

—Psalm 37:1-2

Abundance, as the best Christians see it, comes from the providence of God. Nearly all Western nations have a day of thanksgiving, often connected with the various harvest times of that particular country. God gives good gifts to His children, and Jesus taught us to celebrate those days by being joyous and thankful for our daily bread. Bread and thanksgiving do go together. Who can admire those who are so self-made they feel no need to give thanks to God?

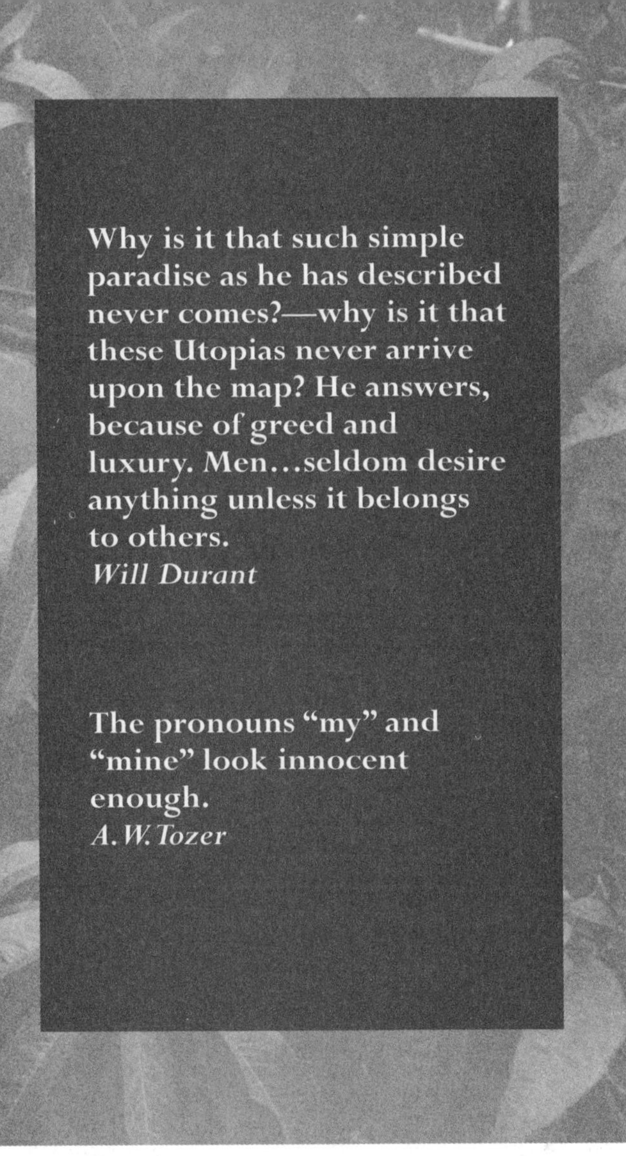

Why is it that such simple paradise as he has described never comes?—why is it that these Utopias never arrive upon the map? He answers, because of greed and luxury. Men...seldom desire anything unless it belongs to others.
Will Durant
The pronouns "my" and "mine" look innocent enough.
A. W. Tozer

Read Psalm 37 noting each comment about the wicked and the righteous. How would you summarize the Psalmist's promise to the humble or righteous?

____

____

____

What does the Psalm promise will happen to the wicked?

____

____

____

Psalm 37, seems to say above all else, "Quit trying to keep up with the Joneses." Great advice along the route to contentment. Contentment is the great gift of God's providence. When we come to understand that all we have has been supplied by a loving God, we will know contentment!

List as many reasons as you can why such understanding can lead to contentment.

____

____

____

Paul could honestly say, "I have learned the secret of being content" (Phil. 4:12), because he had learned that God would meet all his needs "according to His riches in glory in Christ Jesus" (Phil. 4:19). John the Baptist encouraged some hard-driving career soldiers, "Be content with your pay" (Luke 3:14). But in each of these cases, contentment never comes from a sense that anyone can find it in their own paltry human reserves. Real contentment comes in our reliance on the vast treasuries of God.

God does not promise us great wealth, and we must never be guilty of preaching that health and wealth are the results of godliness. We have brothers and sisters in India and Africa who love God with singleness of heart and yet die of starvation. All the wealth these can ever know must arise from the abundance of a faithful heart. Richer are these than those Wall-Street tycoons who keep yachts and mansions but never pray.

What situations tempt you to envy those who ignore God and yet seem to prosper?

What encouragements against envying the wicked does Psalm 37:1-13 provide?

As we examine the Thirty-seventh Psalm, let us approach it by saying that our appreciation for God's abundance grows as we learn a dependency on Him. But our appreciation is also related to our willingness to refuse to keep up with the Joneses. We must strive not to destroy our lives with such materialistic struggles. We must not fret because of the wealth of evildoers. We must give our allegiance to Christ and make God alone our treasury. We must not allow petty sins or cheap indulgences to distract us from our love affair with God.

In C. S. Lewis's *The Great Divorce,* a new ghost arrives at paradise with a lizard on his lapel. The gatekeeper informs him that lizards are not welcome in the New Eden. He must throw the lizard to the ground and stomp it to death. This will demonstrate that his heart is worthy of the new world. The ghost agonizes over his dilemma. He dearly wants entrance into paradise, but the little lizard has long been his intimate friend. How could he give up his fondest preoccupation? Could he bear the separation? Could heaven be heaven without his dear companion?

What Lewis does not say about the lizard—this unrelenting addiction—fascinates me most. The beast has no doubt sprung from his petty indulgences and was so tolerated it at last became his master. This demonic abuser has stayed front and center all through the ghost's lifetime, spoiling his appearance, making its demands, soiling his tunic, burdening him with its fatigue, beguiling him with its scaly ugliness. Still, it has lived there with his permission, lending him security. How, indeed, can he give it up without being alone? The lizard has become the focal point for this poor spiritual neurotic. He has cherished his addiction, which all his life has kept him from great abundance.

We are going to play a game of "name that lizard." List all the "lizards" (behaviors, possessions, addictions) you can.

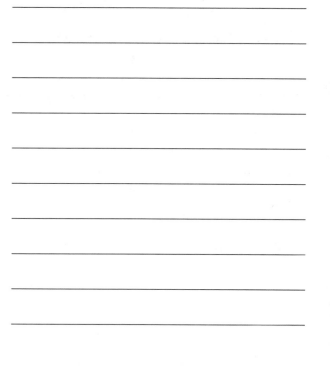

The questions are for us as well. If we abandon our natural dependency, will we find another companion? The man in Lewis's story at last tears the lizard from his clothes and throws it to the ground. Despite its piteous cries for mercy, he crushes it. The corpse of the little beast is then transformed before his eyes. It rises in splendor as a proud steed on which the one-time victim rides through the gates of heaven in triumph. Out of his poverty and renunciation he rides into a new fellowship with the all-powerful Christ.

Briefly describe an example of how you have gained freedom from a "lizard" or how you think it would feel to have such freedom.

____

____

____

How often our petty affection bars us from the treasuries of God's blessings! We cannot arrive at the table of the Holy still clutching our ugly dependence on what the Joneses have. It amounts to nothing when compared to what our Host offers.

Ego is a junk buyer. He hoards trinkets and shops garage sales. He loads us with matchbooks and ticket stubs. He reminisces about our most cherished moments and greatest exhilarations and tells us that this kind of trivia is what matters. He preserves the exact records of those times we felt we had found meaning apart from God. Ego sifts the trash heap of Gehenna daily for baubles that will amuse us. All the while, God has reserved for us the riches that are in Christ Jesus. This is message of Psalm 37.

End your day's study with a time of prayer. Ask God to give you eyes to see His riches and to see through the passing temptations of the world's kind of wealth.

Day 2 HEALTH, WEALTH, AND RUMMAGE SALES

Trust in the L*ORD and do good; dwell in the land*

and enjoy safe pasture. Delight yourself in the L*ORD*

and he will give you the desires of your heart.

—Psalm 37:3-4

Someone asked a visitor to America from a developing country what was the most unforgettable thing she had seen in the West.

Without hesitation she answered, "The size of your garbage cans."

In Calcutta I more than once came across a woman picking up wilted cabbage leaves from the city gutters. I continually rebuke myself for my spending, buying for family members trinkets that only furnish next year's garage sales. Before the eyes of a starving world desperate for even discarded cabbage leaves and and-me-down clothing, I must confess I have become another junk collector in the great "throw-away" society.

In the West we have made consumerism a god, and by the world's standards we are rich. We have it all and cannot conceive of abandoning our immense holdings for God. Yet without a spirit of renunciation we cannot meet the Host at the table He has prepared for us.

The wise heart will relish the riches of self-denial, for that is the only path through the needle's eye: "It is easier for a camel to go through the eye of a needle than for a rich person to enter the kingdom of God," Jesus said (Matt. 19:23-24). The needle's eye is the narrow door to eternal life. We cannot pass through it unless we lay down our cumbersome, egoistic baggage. The needle's eye is the only door to Christ's lordship. In context Jesus' challenge occurred following His encounter with a young man who was the product of wealth and privilege.

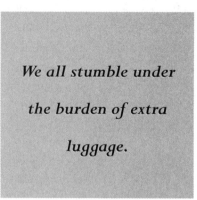

We all stumble under the burden of extra luggage.

What separated the young man from Christ in Matthew 19:16-22?

❑ lack of biblical knowledge
❑ disobedience to the laws of God
❑ possessions that were too important
❑ a controlling and rebellious wife

From most to least powerful, how would you rank the following examples of what Hebrews calls "every weight ... that so easily ensnares us" (Heb. 12:1).

____ sexual temptation
____ desire for material possessions
____ craving for fame and recognition
____ lust for power
____ unwillingness to be disturbed—laziness

You may have ordered those temptations any way that seemed right to you. Is the desire for things a more subtle but constant issue? We all stumble under the burden of extra luggage.

The appetite for having is born in our early years. When my own children were small, they each had their own toy box. They screamed if anyone invaded it. I was making the house payments, providing their food, clothing their bodies. While I provided what they needed, they quarreled over what they didn't need. Rightly does the Bible call us the children of God! Even in the midst of his splendor, we crave and quarrel over our small possessions, remaining all too complacent about what we need most. But when is sacrifice reasonable? How much shall we renounce before our flesh is crucified? We face "the eye of the needle" not once, but continually. Each time we are tempted to buy a new home, new car, new clothes, furniture, or electronic gadgets, we feel anew the tug of war between two kingdoms: the kingdom of God and the kingdom of this world. Is it possible to get on well in both kingdoms at once?

What did Jesus warn us about this double pursuit in Matthew 6:24?

❑ We can't have it both ways.
❑ Deny the flesh and you will become holy.
❑ We should use the riches of this world to build the kingdom of God

The two treasures lie in opposite directions. To move toward ownership in one realm is to disinherit ourselves in the other.

I can hear the protests: Don't the wealthy pray? Don't saints own real estate? There may indeed be examples of both. But they aren't easy to find. We really can't have it both ways. Either we'll cling to God or to our riches.

If (as Psalm 37:4 says) God gives us "the desires of [our] hearts," how shall we ever live up to His call for self-denial? The truth is that God will give us the desires of our hearts as long as our hearts crave Him, and that requires self-denial. We are only true believers when our hearts hunger for the desires that fill the heart of our Savior.

Affluent, Western Christianity often combines swank, Madison-Avenue techniques with gaining spirituality through "reasonable" poverty. Low-demand video churches herald the doctrine that God exists merely to meet our needs and whims but not to order our lives.

How would you respond to a person who said, "God exists to meet our needs ... but not to order our lives"?

____

____

____

____

Many voices in todays "Christian" media try to lead us to believe that Bible study and limited contributions will make us joyful, diseaseless, and rich. No pain is required. No poverty need be endured. Euphoria will come automatically to dispel every barrier to our rosy destiny.

One pyramid-style corporation makes every praying Christian a limited partner and shares the blessings and profits with them. This company claims to base its whole structure on Matthew 6:33: "Seek first the kingdom of God and His righteousness, and *all these things will be provided for you"* (emphasis added).

We would rather own things than be owned by Christ. We believe we will be respected in this world if we "succeed." But do Christians draw people to Christ by their example of success? If so, to what sort of Christ are they drawn? A Christ who enables devout men and women to glory in their possessions and never feel guilty for their indulgence? Thus today we have pitiful, status-occupied disciples, achiever/entrepreneur believers. These "Jesus executives" rule over empires where goods and people are expendable. Thomas Merton said that to the status conscious disciple peace is merely the liberty of exploiting others without any reprisals or interruptions. These double-minded, "successful" Christians may even claim to hate greed. In reality, they only hate the greed in others.

We try in vain to walk around our own inner urge to get ahead in this world while deepening our spiritual connections. John White has captured our dilemma: "We would like to believe that our treasure was in heaven and that heaven was our real choice. But...earthly treasures continue to attract. We may not want outrageous wealth and would be content with reasonable financial security. But we don't want to miss out on anything either. We are ambivalent.... We are like the monkey with his fist trapped inside the coconut shell clutching a fistful of peanuts. The monkey wants freedom and peanuts, and he cannot have both."[1] We are spiritually neurotic, trying to embrace indulgence and renunciation at the same time.

Knowing this ongoing struggle, what are three things you could do to strengthen your grip on Christ and weaken materialism's grip on you?

____

____

____

Krister Stendahl once observed that no prophet ever had a salary. I fear he is right. Simon the magician once tried to pay Peter to purchase the apostle's spiritual powers. Peter's rebuke was, "May your silver be destroyed with you" (Acts 8:20). Pastor Carlyle Marney paraphrased the passage, "To hell with you and your money!"[2] The words are strong, but they center on the priority of discipleship. God calls us beyond the love of money to the adoration of His Son.

Day 3 RENUNCIATION PAST AND PRESENT

Commit your way to the LORD; trust in him and he will do this: He will make your righteousness shine like the dawn, the justice of your cause like the noonday sun.—Psalm 37:5-6

This great verse answers the unsolved riddle of yesterday's lesson. If we trust in the Lord, our desires will be to him. What God wants with us, we will want for us.

I am convinced that God does not want the huge material inequities that exist in our world. I find nothing fair in the fact that we Americans (6 percent of the global population) consume half of the world's fuel and food. Surely this is not acceptable to a God who loves the whole world equally. But we have grown accustomed to the inequity because it provides us with all the indulgences we love. Never has there been a time when the wealthy evangelical church in America more certainly needs to hear her Savior saying, "if anyone wants to come with Me, he must deny himself, take up his cross daily, and follow Me" (Luke 9:23).

But we are wealthy, and our purses are so heavy that we cannot carry both our goods and His gallows. So we cling to our wallets and leave the cross bearing to those who have less to surrender. Somehow we would like to find a way to achieve godliness without repudiating wealth.

Identify a time when you gave up your "goods" to follow Christ.

____

____

____

How does it feel to know the smile of God because we've put Him first?

____

____

Would you describe yourself today as—

- ❑ more willing than ever before to sacrifice to follow Christ
- ❑ about as willing to sacrifice for the kingdom as in my earlier years
- ❑ less willing to give up my treasures to follow Christ

Our battle seems set against nature itself. Our appetites are so much a part of us! To hunger for inwardness in a consumer world marks us as odd and out of step with those around us. We have generally been taught that fanatics close themselves in solitude. We are afraid of being called prudes or puritans. We are afraid our friends will draw away.

Prudes and puritans follow a grim Jehovah, gray and severe, who forbids laughter. Howard Hendricks once defined a puritan as a person who suffers from an overwhelming dread that somewhere, sometime, somehow, someone may be enjoying himself.

Which is the greater dread for you?

- ❑ the fear of being thought a prude
- ❑ the fear of giving up some precious possession
- ❑ the fear of losing intimacy with Christ

We want to live with good, godly priorities, but without criticism. We want to renounce without waving our renunciation in the face of those who would misunderstand it. We need to remember that the best of this world's models of renunciation dressed in burlap and were called extremists.

Which of the following would be most difficult for you?

❑ giving up my material possessions
❑ fear that people would think me an extremist
❑ fear that things would separate me from Christ
❑ knowing God's will about what to give away and what to keep

Read the story about Thomas à Becket below and then write what you consider to be the greatest lesson from his life. Plan to share your statement with your group.

Thomas à Becket wore the crown of the State before he wore the miter of the church. But two facts stand out about the martyred Archbishop of Canterbury. First, he took the part of poor priests against the interests of the wealthy hierarchy. But even more impressive was his close identification with the poor, discovered only after his murder. The poor priests who prepared his body for burial found that underneath his regalia, he was clad in the simple haircloth of a country monk. The priests celebrated the consecration of the dead archbishop by breaking into joy at worship: "Then the monks wholly transformed with spiritual joy, lifted their hearts and hands to heaven, glorifying God. They gave over sorrow for rejoicing, and turned their laments to cries of gladness."[3]

What lesson do you draw from the testimony of Thomas à Becket?

____

____

Once Francis turned to the disciplined life, he became interested in justice for the poor.

Psalm 37 beckons us to trade our little desires for the spiritual wealth that awaits us when we surrender to God. Various traditions surround the conversion of Francis of Assisi. In the Zeffirelli film *Brother Sun, Sister Moon,* Francis repudiates his father's wealth in a most unusual way. Standing in the square of Assisi, while the townspeople look on, he takes off his father's rich robes and turns his naked body to the sunny fields where the lepers and poor live as outcasts. The townspeople look away in a kind of capitalistic embarrassment as Francis says with determination, "I am born again."

Such a statement about the new birth cannot be equated with the evangelical cliché. Francis does not come to conversion after reading a religious tract. He arrives at his utter renovation of life and values by submitting his soul to God. To possess the treasure in the field, Saint Francis sold all. He had confronted the needle's eye and won. He banqueted at the wilderness table. But his renunciation had its consequences. Most of the people in Assisi thought it a shame for such a talented and wealthy young man to throw his life away.

But notice this: Once Francis turned to the disciplined life, he became interested in justice for the poor. Isn't this the precise message of Psalm 37:6? The providence of God, properly understood, furnished Francis with a meat the world had never tasted, an abundance too glorious for bank accounts or stock options. Jesus knew this meat too. When His disciples brought Him bread, He informed them, "I have food to eat that you don't know about" (John 4:32).

Imagine that triumphant moment when Thomas à Kempis finished *The Imitation of Christ.* He refused to sign his name to it. For him, it was an offering to the inner Christ. It wasn't so much that he refused to acknowledge the work. Rather, the fullness he knew in Christ dissolved his need for recognition. E. M. Forster once said that whenever our words are truly significant, a signature only detracts from the significance. The ego quickly scratches its gaudy signature over all insignificant art and runs about displaying the piece, crying, "Mine. Mine. Mine!"

Under what kinds of circumstances does your ego most often show up?

____

____

____

____

____

Thomas à Kempis had learned a great independence from the demanding, even voracious, appetite for approval. Hearing applause is like drinking seawater; it creates an ever more insatiable thirst for itself. Those addicted to their own popularity often finish life with an alkaline emptiness.

Are there more contemporary examples of renunciation? Only rarely do we see men and women in our day reaching for it. Charlotte (Lottie) Diggs Moon, a Baptist missionary to China, starved to death because she used her salary to feed the Chinese during a famine. Nate Saint gave his life for the spreading of the gospel in the twentieth century. These are powerful examples of those who, on every mission field, are performing tireless and thankless service because their treasure is hidden in another world.

Corrie ten Boom, both before and after her concentration camp experience during the Holocaust, reached out to help all she could. Before her imprisonment, she helped Jews. After the war she worked with refugees and with the mentally disabled, taking them into her home for whatever ministry they required. She initiated a rehabilitation center for war victims in Buchenwald that still ministers to people in need.

How have you seen believers giving up their material goods to follow Christ?

____

____

____

____

____

Do you think they are more or less fulfilled for their decisions? Why?

____

____

____

____

____

____

End your day's study with a time of prayer. Ask God what He would have you to renounce in order to experience glorious freedom in Him. If you are unwilling to pry your fingers from your possessions, ask Him for a willing heart.

Day 4 NO COMPARISON

Be still before the Lord *and wait patiently for him;*

do not fret when men succeed in their ways, when

they carry out their wicked schemes.—Psalm 37:7

How much of our lives we spend worrying about whether the world is under-succeeding or over-succeeding us. The psalmist warns us against all such neurotic comparisons. We must not try to think well of ourselves by comparing ourselves with those we know.

Do you think we are more tormented by what we have or what others have that we don't have? Explain.

In most churches, ministry is limited by socioeconomics. Many years ago Peter Wagner of Fuller Theological Seminary said that churches grew by adding homogeneous units. This high-sounding blending of the Great Commission with sociology really means that, for the most part, Christianity in the West has not broken free from economic fetters. Thus it cannot become the kind of church it should be.

But the fault is not uniquely Western. It is a worldwide human frailty. I was once confessing my disenchantment with suburban churchmanship to a friend who ministers in the Third World. I lamented that some of my members who live in $200,000 homes enjoy more status in the church than those in $100,000 homes. "How I wish I could serve in your country, where poverty has reduced all to one common denominator," I told him.

"Not so fast," he admonished me. "In your parish a $200,000 homeowner may look down on a $100,000 homeowner, but in my country families who live in two packing crates look down on those confined to one."

While I was visiting Mexico City some time ago, the comfortable home I stayed in overlooked a wretchedly poor section of the city. Their dwellings textured the hillside with slums. One small tarpaper shack rested above a dugout in the hillside. A single, thin electrical wire led into the tarpaper shack. "Do you see that wire?" asked my host. "The family that lives in that shack has electricity. I've watched them for a long time, and I've never seen them speak to the family that lives in the dugout beneath them."

What does this story tell you about human nature and possessions?

Merely ridding ourselves of possessions is not enough. Renunciation is a matter of the heart. Having is a kind of venom that makes us monsters with status. It takes so little to make us believe we are better than those with less. But our emphasis on being must always exceed our emphasis on having.

Which of the following do you think best fits Jesus' parable in Matthew 20:1-15?

❑ Comparing yourself with others is a route to misery.
❑ God is not fair, but He is good.
❑ Grace demands that we forego comparing ourselves with others
❑ Don't worry; be happy.

How does Psalm 37 help to explain what Jesus meant in the parable of the workers in the vineyard?

____

____

____

The gospel does not elevate a mere lack of money. The poor are not to be revered because they are poor. Christ chose to leave heaven not because he despised the riches of glory or adored the poverty of earth. Renunciation was not the point of the Incarnation. His earthly poverty didn't make him Savior and Lord. His willingness to submit himself to the Father did.

Who did Jesus say was blessed (Matt. 5:3)?

____

Wealth is not the psalmist's point, nor is poverty Jesus' point. Poverty of spirit is, and with that there is no comparison. Humbling oneself in obedience to God is positive renunciation. We acknowledge our need, our emptiness, and we are the better for it.

Louis Evely confessed that as he grew older, he came to understand the great blessings of poverty. It was not to be avoided but exalted: "We all carry the same burden.... Each one groans and sighs beneath a weight that is just a little more than he can carry. He is obliged to acknowledge his poverty. He has need of another. He has need of all the others to help him bear it. The burden that we ourselves bear reveals the burden that is borne by everyone else. Our misery is fraternal; it teaches us about others; it introduces us into the great fraternity of the poor."[4]

The poverty of those beneath the cross creates in them a need for Christ. His inner presence becomes for them the only wealth that matters. Let us not miss the true glory of Psalm 37. The psalmist has chosen patient waiting for God. Keeping up with the Joneses has lost its control in his life.

How do you think it would feel to be totally free from the concern to "keep up with the Joneses?"

____

____

____

Write a prayer asking God to lead you to such freedom.

____

____

____

____

____

____

____

How much my understanding grows with the years! When first I received God's gift of grace, I thought my best gift to him would be what I owned. During my teenage years, I shared freely the little wages I received. I had been well taught by my world: Money was the great possession; to share it freely was to show great love. But the psalmist would tell us forthrightly, "Wait patiently" (v. 7). Put your ambition in perspective. The way to release your soul from the clutches of materialism is to renounce not just your attempt to get ahead but your need to get ahead.

How false my first ideas of renunciation were! My best gift was the gift of myself, given in many years of service to others. It wasn't so much that I had renounced some other pursuit or life-consuming career. Rather, I had such a desire to follow Christ in ministry that I never saw at all the great gift I had been giving. All who have eaten at the table of inwardness have passed by lesser meals. But they never noticed because of their delight with the taste of a different kind of meat, beside which earthly feasts pale in comparison: the presence of the Holy.

Day 5 SPELLBOUND BY THE SAVIOR

The days of the blameless are known to the LORD,

and their inheritance will endure forever. . . .

If the LORD delights in a man's way, he makes

his steps firm; though he stumble, he will not fall,

for the LORD upholds him with his hand.

—Psalm 37:18,23-24

In the last analysis, the Thirty-seventh Psalm shows us that the Lord's true delight is not in the wealth a person may be able to accumulate. The Lord takes pride in the soul's obedience. It is not how much you own but how well you follow. Such obedience will meet the firm, upholding hand of God.

At the Sea of Galilee, Christ called to the disciples to follow him. And so they did, leaving behind their boats and businesses. They were so taken with Christ that they never felt the cost of their renunciation. They walked in the epicenter of a new adoration that had silently slain their old affections. Renunciation that is self-aware is mere asceticism, subtly boasting its own magnificent sacrifice. The apostles surrendered the possessions that stood between them and the will of God, yet we do not remember them because they chose poverty but because they adored Christ.

Mark the following *true* or *false* on the basis of the paragraph above.

___ 1. If we focus on our self sacrifice it becomes merely human effort.

___ 2. Loving Christ passionately makes other desires less important.

___ 3. We admire the apostles primarily for all they gave up to follow Christ.

___ 4. Human effort boasts about all it has given up to serve God.

If we too are spellbound by Christ's excellence, relinquishment will be more a by-product of devotion than a prerequisite to it. True lovers of Christ can stand the pain of self-denial. They exemplify Gandhi's great truth, "Renounce and enjoy." The glory of the Spirit blinds them to the showy, temporal treasures of earth. They see only Christ. His hands are bruised and scarred as they now break the loaf that allows them to share in communion with the Holy. All but the third answer above were true.

As guests at His table, we must turn from a once-selfish life to seek the higher life. Our Host has no ambition but to do the Father's bidding. He could not fail at life, because life held nothing for Him. So our lives must be lived in imitation of the Holy. At Gethsemane Christ struggled with selfish desire. Now we must come to our own Gethsemane and there drink the cup of the Father's will. Then our obedience will commend us. Then, says the psalmist, even though we stumble, we will not fall.

Philippians 2:1-8 is worth long meditation on how Christ emptied himself. Following our Lord's example, our walk with him is to be a continuing cycle of emptying and filling. A bucket will carry water in direct proportion to the degree of its emptiness when it is lowered into the well. If there are rocks in the bucket, it will not be able to bring up as much water. Send an empty bucket down the shaft, and the filling will be more complete.

Christ could not fail at life, because life held nothing for Him.

Once Thomas Edward Brown was walking along a beach when he reached down and picked up a seashell. As he put the shell to his ear to hear its version of the sea, he was startled as the spidery legs of a sand crab reached out of the opening. When the old mollusk had died, the crab moved into the vacant shell. This prompted Brown to meditate on the riddle of the indwelling life, and he wrote these verses:

If thou couldst empty all thyself of self,
Like to a shell dishabited,
Then might He find thee on the Ocean shelf,
And say—"This is not dead,"—
And fill thee with Himself instead.
But thou art all replete with very thou
And hast such shrewd activity
Then, when He comes, He says:—"This is enow
Unto itself—'Twere better let it be:
It is so small and full, there is no room for Me."[5]

We need to pass through the needle's eye and find our place at the lonely table. Our self-denial must become our way of life. Let it not be a showy sacrifice or a boisterous brag, but a quiet turning from our own concern. In self-rebuke, let us listen to the Lord of the Apocalypse: "You say, 'I'm rich; I have become wealthy, and need nothing, and you don't know that you are wretched, pitiful, poor, blind, and naked. I advise you to buy from Me gold refined in the fire so that you may be rich, and white clothes so that you may be dressed and your shameful nakedness not be exposed, and ointment to spread on your eyes so that you may see" (Rev. 3:17-18).

Think of two people you know, one who makes a show of religion and every sacrifice for Jesus and one who has a vibrant faith that results in a quiet turning from his or her concern. What do you think makes them different?

____

____

____

____

____

____

After Christ said it was easier for a camel to pass through the eye of a needle than for a rich man to enter heaven, the apostles asked, "Who then can be saved?" Their astonishment is appropriate. By keeping the laws, even by giving all to the poor, one cannot be saved. "With man this is impossible," Jesus replied, "but with God all things are possible" (Matt. 19:26). We cannot save ourselves by our own renunciation. But as the Spirit of Christ works in us, his handiwork is manifest. Could the difference in the two people you considered be that one has works while the other has fruit?

And when all things take their proper place, the towering Christ of the Apocalypse presents himself as our intimate friend. The provident God of Psalm 37 does indeed fill our needs. Are we disappointed with God? Never. We are alone at the table, and he smiles across as if to say, "I have brought you through the needle's eye. And since you have been faithful with these few things, I will make you ruler over many."

Describe a time when God has met your needs.

____

____

____

____

____

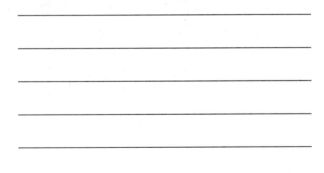

What would you say to those who are disappointed with God?

____

____

____

Write your own paraphrase of Psalm 37:25.

____

____

____

All that we might have boils down to a matter of faith. "Without faith," said the writer of the Book of Hebrews, "it is impossible to please God" (Heb. 11:6). But the righteous will never be forsaken, and God honors their righteousness with his abundance, ordinarily. Bread is not an automatic corollary of righteousness, but God would have all his hungry children fed.

It has been my experience, through seasons of faithfulness, that I have not seen God's beloved faithful go hungry. And at every plea for bread, I personally have met his abundance. God is truly the giver of all good things, and his gifts are more than abundant for those who trust.

[1]John White, *The Golden Cow* (Downers Grove, IL: InterVarsity Press, 1979), 47–48.

[2]Carlyle Marney, *Priests to Each Other* (Valley Forge: Judson, 1974), 94.

[3]Richard Winston, *Thomas à Becket* (London: Constable, 1967), 361, quoted in Eddie Ensley, Sounds of Wonder (New York: Paulist, 1977), 69.

[4]Louis Evely, *We Are All Brothers* (New York: Doubleday, 1975).

[5]Thomas Edward Brown, "Indwelling," in James Stephens, Edwin L. Beck, and Royall H. Snow, eds., *Victorian and Later English Poets* (New York: American Book Co., 1934).

WEEK 4 THE UNFORSAKING CHRIST

Day 1 BORN WITH CHRIST

My God, my God, why have you forsaken me?

—Psalm 22:1

Nothing stabs at faith like the silence of God. When we feel we must have His nearness to live, and yet He seems to stand a great distance away, we beg Him to draw closer. Still, to question the unforsaking presence of God is humanity's lot. In Psalm 22, David the king is caught in such a despairing mood. He doubts the steadfast presence of God.

Read Psalm 22. Check David's responses that you have identified with most closely at some point in your life.

- ❑ despair at the silence of God (v. 1-2)
- ❑ review of God's historic faithfulness (v. 4-5)
- ❑ self loathing language (v. 6)

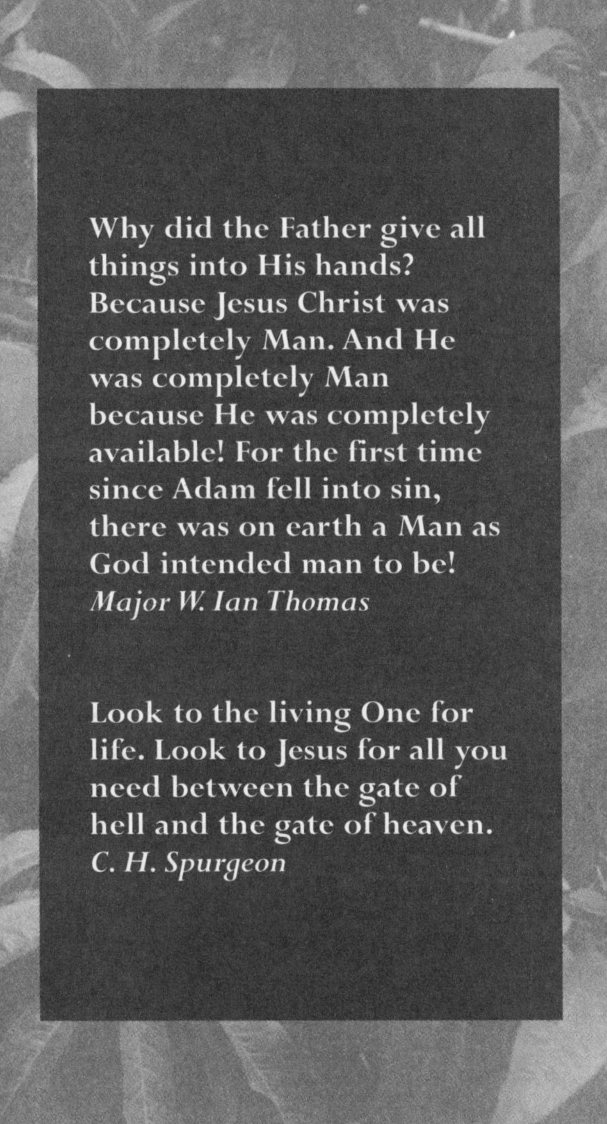

Why did the Father give all things into His hands? Because Jesus Christ was completely Man. And He was completely Man because He was completely available! For the first time since Adam fell into sin, there was on earth a Man as God intended man to be!
Major W. Ian Thomas
Look to the living One for life. Look to Jesus for all you need between the gate of hell and the gate of heaven.
C. H. Spurgeon

- ❑ self-pity because of mistreatment (v. 7-8,16-17)
- ❑ bargaining with God (v. 22)
- ❑ preaching faith to others (v. 23)
- ❑ ultimate conclusion of faith (v. 29-31)

David once experienced the sweet intimacy of Psalm 23—the holy table. Now the Psalmist is traveling through the valley of the shadow, and David's seeming loss of God's presence in the struggles of life feels like more than he can bear.

Is the God who promised to be with him really with him? David cries out his neediness, but God seems silent. His despair is utter.

If you have experienced a time when God seemed silent, what was the most difficult part of that time?

____

____

____

____

On the cross Jesus felt David's despair and actually quoted from Psalm 22. But the psalmist was not thinking only of death when he wrote these words. He was considering the whole of life. In a sense, the entirety of our lives properly begins with being born. But from the moment we are born, we begin to die. When we are old enough, each of us can look back on our life and see that it is a single piece of existence.

Birth is a drama in which the spotlights fall only on a simple cast of two. In her aloneness, the mother bears down on the blue-white edges of her existence. There, in the dark, behind clenched eyelids, is her impatient longing, her crying out for the life within her own to be set free. Suddenly, that inner life splits forth; and in brilliance, the symbiotic oneness cuts forth to the wholeness of two. The mother's anguish dissolves into joy at the sound of an infant's voice.

If we could recall the heaving of our births, we should bless the natural force that shoved us rudely into independence. The warm softness that enveloped our waiting was stripped to unkind exposure. Dark and heavy circumstance folded in on us, moving us against our will. The stricture of our inverted journey was a vise of strangling and painful closeness. We became compressed, shoved, contorted. We were finally forced forward, downward, and life-ward. All the while, in this dark process was a golden glory waiting for the anguish to die. Then light spilt across our unfocused souls, and we were free, free, *free!*

How does the drama of birth picture both the hopefulness and despair of life?

hopefulness: ________________________________

____

____

despair: ________________________________

____

____

The process of natural birth becomes the center of Jesus' metaphor in John 3:7 when He says you must be "born again." Indeed, we must be!

In the following paragraph underline the words or phrases that compare physical with spiritual birth.

The pain of spiritual birth closely resembles the pain of our natural birth. We are reluctant to venture into God's new life, for it is a radical, new kind of existence. We are pressed by the overwhelming dread of our sin. But the time of birth has come. We move along a strange path we barely understand, for we have never traveled it before. The heavy walls of self-doubt and inner confusion constrict in strangling closeness. Why, why, why, God? Why this pain? Why the black mirror of repentance that makes us see ourselves as we are? We cry in the unsure, unfocused, crushing void. Yet it is a warm darkness that aches for the anguish to die. There is a washing of inner light. God cuts the long umbilical cord that bound us to dying. Life rises like a phoenix from the ashes of things confessed and forgiven. We are *born again.* And what is this golden glory? It is the moment of birth, the gift at the end of our waiting.

Now we belong to Christ. For the first time, we love and adore the holy one who labored to bring us to life. He has awaited our coming with steadfast love, and we are drawn to Him as an injured child reaches for his parents' embrace.

But the initial warmth of our God-relationship all too soon runs into despair. Are we born again? Is His love steadfast? It hardly seems so. It seems our cries for grace in the deepest seasons of our need meet only a dark silence. The presence is absent. The hope is despair. The fatherly warmth of the Abba God seems to give way to the arctic air of nihilism. And how the absence aches.

Draw a graph of either your first year as a believer or a longer graph of your relationship with God. Start with the period before you embraced Christ.

Does your graph reflect the description in the preceding paragraph? I suspect that most of us experience an initial euphoria followed by some degree of letdown. David knew this aching absence. In the first portion of the Psalm he has passed the point where any of his earthly friends can offer him help in making sense of his grief. His despair has become so deep that he no longer senses that God is on his side. It seems to him that God has forsaken him. Tomorrow we will explore more of David's journey with the times when God seems achingly silent.

End today's study by reflecting on how your life with Christ has been similar and/or different than David's. Record your thoughts below.

____

____

____

____

Day 2 THE CHRIST WHO IS LIKE US

Why are you so far from saving me, so far from the words of my groaning?—Psalm 22:1

The great glory of our faith is the name Immanuel, for God, in Christ, came to us. The glory of this truth is that He is not only with us in our times of jubilee, but He is with us in our times of despair.

When the nails were in His hands Jesus quoted David: "My God, my God, why have You forsaken me?" (Matt. 27:46,) How wonderful that on the cross Jesus should quote the very words we all too often cry in our seasons of despair.

When you experience despair or suffering, how does Jesus' quote from the cross make you feel?

____

____

____

____

Fill in the blanks from Heb. 2:18 and 4:15 (HCSB)

Since He Himself was tested and has ____________,

He is able to help those who are ______________.

For we do not have a high priest who is unable to

____________ with our weaknesses, but One who

has been ____________ in every way as we are, yet was without sin.

Who then is this Christ? Is He not our fellow struggler in the hard times? He is the Immanuel Christ. Like us, living with our humanity, Christ taught us about God and revealed to us our own human need. As God, Christ can meet our needs, but as a human He understands them. Jesus is never a stranger to our despair, for He has faced the futility of purely earthly living.

Sergei Kourdakov, a persecutor of Christians under a dreadful regime, finally faced up to the facts: Those he killed for their faith had greater reasons for dying than he had for living! After he came to glorious faith, he wrote: "The words [of Christ] grabbed my heart. I was somehow frightened and uneasy, like a man walking on unfamiliar ground. . . . Something deep within me, some tiny ember of humanity was still alive somewhere inside me."[1]

How did the apostle Paul view life and death according to Phil 1:21?

❑ Utterly meaningless! Everything is meaningless.
❑ God is in His heaven, and all is right with the world.
❑ While willing to live for Christ he longed to go and be with his Savior
❑ All things work together for good for those called according to God's purpose.

In what sense do you have more reason to die with Christ than to live without Him?

____

____

____

Kourdakov became a Christian because he was touched by what Christ places in the hearts of all who believe. This substance enables believers to shake their fists in the face of despair and order light into the soul's worst gloom. We too may go to Jesus because He once felt the pain of Psalm 22:1. The Christ who can face such despair must certainly be the Christ for us.

Christ enables believers to shake their fists in the face of despair

Our hymns often celebrate Christ's humanness. "What a friend we have in Jesus." "I've found a friend, O such a friend." "Put your hand in the hand of the man from Galilee." "Man of sorrows, what a name."

What songs speak to you of Jesus' friendship and humanity? Plan to share your list in your group.

____

____

____

____

____

____

____

I wish I could hear you share the songs that minister Christ's love to you. At the table, we share a holy meal with the human Christ, even as our awareness of His godhood grows. He is truly our personal Savior. At the table, we sit together as friends. He is not ashamed of His humanity or of ours. Indeed, His humanity becomes the bridge between His holy Father and us. His godhood redeems, but His manhood makes heaven and earth friends.

At the psalmist's table, God is not lofty and throne-bound on a glittering dais. All pageantry fades. How can we help but love the Son of God who stooped to identify with us without resenting our despair? Novelist Dorothy Sayers said it well when she wrote: "He can exact nothing from man that he has not exacted from himself. He has himself gone through the whole of human experience, from the trivial irritations of family life and the cramping restrictions of hard work and lack of money to the worst horrors of pain and humiliation, defeat, despair, and death. When he was a man, he played the man … and thought it well worthwhile."[2]

God might have been an egotist with no regard for us lower life forms. Instead, He lavished the world with a love second only to that He poured out on His Son (John 3:16). The great Jehovah, secure in the heavens, without a trace of condescension, stepped into Bethlehem. In that one long step down, humanity took a long step up, and God and humankind fell into one long, redeeming embrace.

Using simple language, write a prayer expressing your present feelings to the great creator God who comes and sits with you at the wilderness table.

____

____

____

____

Day 3 THE CHRIST OF THE REAL WORLD

Oh, my God, I cry out by day, but you do not answer, by night, and am not silent. Yet, you are enthroned as the Holy One; you are the praise of Israel. In you our fathers put their trust; they trusted and you delivered them. They cried to you and were saved; in you they trusted and were not disappointed.

—Psalm 22:2-5

A deep wound afflicts the psalmist as he cries out to God for understanding. What is happening in his heart happens also in ours when we focus too much on our own troubles. Our troubles have a way of multiplying as we give them space in our hearts. Our focus on our own despair is all too prone to exaggeration. In other words, we paint our despair darker than it is. We don't mean to do this, it's just that our woes so overwhelm us that we come to regard them as the only problems of any consequence anywhere in the world. Why? Because we focus too much on our own selves. "Woe is me!" becomes the central cry of our self-concern.

Have you experienced a time in the past when some problem has crowded out your horizon so that it became all that you could see?
❑ yes ❑ no **If so, looking back, why do you think the problem loomed so large?**

____

____

____

Most of our pity parties are sparsely attended. Were we to invite anyone else to attend, they might get honest and force us to consider our desperation as a matter of small consequence. We don't want our troubles to be small. After all, it makes us seem trivial too. Frankly, we want to suffer for a little while. How else shall we get the "now, now dearies" we so crave?

Rate your tendency related to self-pity by putting a check mark on the scale below.

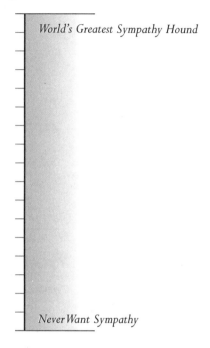

So perhaps the psalmist has deepened his problem because he lacked perspective. He began to compare his sad lot with those he felt had gotten a better deal in life than he had. It appears to David that, in spite of the fact that these people had caused his suffering, God is blessing them: "They cried to you and were saved; in you they trusted and were not disappointed" (Ps. 22:5).

How does it feel when it seems that God is blessing those who have harmed you or someone you love?

____

____

____

____

____

____

Further, we always face the danger that in looking up from our self-pity, we might find someone worse off than we are; then we might be forced to forfeit our narrow preoccupation with our own misery. Viktor Frankl, the famed Jewish Austrian psychiatrist spoke candidly of his marriage in the late 1930s.

In those years, Frankl said that he and his wife used to argue about the most inconsequential sorts of domestic problems. But after only one day in the death camp of Auschwitz, Frankl realized that by comparison, he had never really had any problems.

Perhaps the psalmist deepened his problem because he lacked perspective.

The king is bewildered that God is blessing his enemies. David, who so earnestly sought and delighted in God's presence, felt abandoned. In essence, he cries out, "C'mon God, play fair!" Blinded by his pain and sorrow, David couldn't see that God was playing fair. The psalmist was not alone. The Holy One had prepared a table before David, even in the presence of his enemies. God was there. The Host had never left the table.

In the following paragraph, underline each benefit that comes from knowing Jesus Christ personally.

God calls us to a table of holiness where Jesus himself is the host. The Christ who sits at our table is, of course, much more than a mere man. Jesus is the revealer of a reality so real, it cannot be seen or touched or heard. Beholding our Immanuel Host as one of us, we are gripped by the mystery of all that lies beyond us. This physical world can be miserable. Yet Jesus is our great bridge to another reality. Earth was His, and heaven is His. With Him, I know that God is as real as the air I breathe. I am set free from one-dimensional thinking. I am free from the limits of my despair. I am a citizen of an exciting kingdom "where moth nor rust destroys, and where thieves don't break in and steal" (Matt. 6:20). Christ liberates me from my bondage to the individual moments that compose the brief years of my life. In Him, I live forever. I surpass time.

Describe a time when you have experienced some of these benefits.

____

____

____

____

____

Time is a glutton. It chokes down the years while we whimper. The entire universe is forced to hurry into death. We protest. But sooner or later, we are gone. Our lives are "swifter than a weaver's shuttle" (Job 7:6). Shakespeare said that life is a "poor player that struts and frets his hour upon the stage and then is heard no more."[3] The psalmist also recognizes that he is a prisoner of his dismal time.

Yet for all our protests against its passing, there is never enough time. The whole creation is subject to the tyrant of time. Virginia Stem Owens, a splendid Christian writer of our day, explains the extent of its tyranny:

> *The heart of a shrew, like that of many small, furry animals, beats up to 800 times a minute. Such creatures experience more in an hour than we do in a day. They would laugh at our idea of what constitutes flying time. For them the present is a smaller portion, a hundredth of a second; a day is like a year. Their whole lifetime passes in a matter of months. If time runs out so much faster for small mammals than for us, think of fruit flies measuring their generations in days. Or exotic elements produced in cyclotrons whose existence is measured in thousandths of a second.*[4]

The natural world breaks as symphony and miracle all around us. Yet for all its wonder, it is temporary. As the Savior calls us to the reality of a more permanent world, He frees us from our despair with a positive promise: "Everyone who lives and believes in Me will never die—ever" (John 11:26).

In Psalm 22:3-5, the psalmist once again utters his confidence in the God of Israel. God, he proclaims, was faithful in the past. He can be counted on to be faithful again. Like the poet, we often need our backward glances at the faithfulness of God so we can trust His future faithfulness.

Imagine yourself having crossed over to the reality of heaven. From that vantage point how would your life today look different?

____

____

____

____

____

What advice do you think you would write back to yourself from that shore?

____

____

____

____

____

____

____

John Woolman, the early Quaker sage, said that this world's goods cloud our vision of the other world. Jesus constantly denied Himself and preached that those who did not deny themselves could not be His disciples (Luke 9:23). The wilderness table is a meeting of two who share a common denial. The Savior denied Himself and finished His pilgrimage more than two thousand years ago. Only those who have died to self can behold the reality of the next world. Helen Keller once remarked that the things that cannot be seen or felt are the real things. All else is transient. Look back with the psalmist. Will not the God who was faithful in times past be faithful yet in times to come? Of course. Alive in God, we can know that the glorious faithfulness of God precedes us, looming ahead of us as a sunrise.

Day 4 THE CHRIST WHO COMPLETES US

But I am a worm and not a man, scorned by men and despised by the people. All who seek me mock me; they hurl insults, shaking their heads. He trusts in the L*ORD; let the* L*ORD rescue him. Let him deliver him, since he delights in him.—Psalm 22:6-8*

Self-pity often results in a kind of self-flagellation. Crying, "poor me," we love abusing our psyches. We seem to glory in calling ourselves, as the psalmist puts it, "worms." The obvious cure for those who feel they are being scorned is to ask why people are hurling insults in their direction.

There are times when being mocked is the evidence of a courageous stand. But in other cases, being mocked may be more illusory than real. It may arise from a season of negative inwardness—a dour focus on ourselves. It may result from comparing ourselves with others who seem to have it better than we do.

What bad amusement the game of comparison makes! It inevitably leads to misery. This misery arises from the fact that we don't just compare ourselves with one other person; we usually set our best personal strengths against the best assets of a dozen other people. Naturally, they exceed us handily. Comparing ourselves one at a time would yield a better result.

Which way do you tend to compare yourself?

- ❑ against people I perceive as inferior so I feel proud
- ❑ against people I perceive as superior so I feel depressed
- ❑ some of both
- ❑ neither

How would it change your life if you could avoid all temptations to compare yourself to others?

____

____

____

____

We would find a better peace by dropping all comparisons. Then we might sit with Christ at the table in the wilderness and find our worth in His esteem alone. In His completeness, the Christ of the table reminds us of our soul's finished nobility—our final state of being conformed to the image of Christ (Rom. 12:2). In the perfect presence of Him who knew no sin (2 Cor. 5:21), we then will behold our imperfection. We will move at last with hope into His eternal presence, and our union with Him will be complete.

Rate yourself on a scale of 1 to 10 for how far you have come in completing each of the discipleship tasks in the paragraph you just read.

____ 1. I primarily find my worth in His esteem alone.
____ 2. I celebrate my soul's finished nobility in Christ.
____ 3. I am conscious of my imperfection.
____ 4. I am moving with hope into His eternal presence and experiencing my union with Him.

Our marvelous Christ fosters a yearning in us to become like Him. He doesn't do this by ordering us to behave ourselves or try to be better. He certainly doesn't play the comparison game. He doesn't beat us down with pain and sorrow so we will become humbled and whipped spirits. Rather, He gives us a hunger to become more like Him. And He delights to feed this hunger: "The poor will eat and be satisfied; they who seek the Lord will praise him" (Ps. 22:26). This is our destiny, for when we see Him in eternity, "we will be like Him" (1 John 3:2).

Go back to the exercise above where you rated your progress. Forget your performance. Talk to the Father about what He has been doing in your life. Praise Him for the hunger He is developing in you.

We are the not-yet beings. We will never be satisfied until we come to the completion Christ has in mind. As the Holy One once created us physically, He is now recreating us in the circumstances of our lives. But we can be confident that "the sufferings of this present time are not worth comparing with the glory that is going to be revealed to us" (Rom. 8:18).

'Tis the Master who holds the mallet,
And day by day
He is chipping whatever environs
The form away;
Which, under His skillful cutting,
He means shall be
Wrought silently out to beauty
Of such degree
Of faultless and full perfection,
That angel eyes
Shall look on the finished labor
With new surprise,
That even His boundless patience
Could grave His own
Features upon such fractured
And stubborn stones.[6]

God is now dealing with the not-yet-ness of our lives. Paul told the Philippians that he was confident that He who had begun a good work in them would "carry it on to completion until the day of Christ Jesus" (Phil. 1:6).

The psalmist is cast down because he finds so little esteem for his faith. His enemies slur God for what appears to them to be God's unfaithfulness:

"All who see me mock me;
they hurl insults, shaking their heads:
'He trusts in the LORD;
let the LORD rescue him.
Let him deliver him,
since he delights in him' "(Ps. 22:7-8).

Will God deliver His hurting child? Sometimes, when we behold the suffering of the best of souls, we wonder. But God is there—as elusive as He is near. He never slumbers. His deliverance is on the way. We will be lifted up above our defeat. At some hour of our lives, He always wins; and when He wins, we win.

We unfinished saints, are intolerant of other unfinished saints.

Have you lived with Christ long enough to see Him bring victory from the suffering of one of His godly children? ❑ yes ❑ no ❑ I'm not sure.

If so, describe an example: ____________________

____

____

____

____

Yet a sad impiety runs rampant through the church. Without any regard to true holiness, we confess, "I'm living a pretty good life!" At least in this case, the psalmist never does this. He does not grow arrogant before God, boasting, "Look what an outstanding person I am. How can you treat your friends the way you do?" Such pride issues from a dangerous relativism. We define holiness by comparing our morality with that of others. At the table of Psalm 23, we are not so haughty. In the presence of our Host, we never congratulate ourselves in the form of spiritual arrogance. There at His table, we "hunger and thirst for righteousness" (Matt. 5:6).

Merely going to church cannot nurture that hunger. We are far more likely to discover the shortcomings of others than to see them in ourselves. We, the unfinished saints, are intolerant of other unfinished saints. We are prone to accuse God for not making people more like Jesus after He saves them. Actually, we are not offended that others live lives so unpleasing to Christ, but rather that they displease us.

What shortcomings in your own life might you have never seen if you had not been confronted by them in the lives of others?

____

____

____

____

Early in my ministry, I was discouraged that many in my congregation were "unlike Jesus." I grew spiritually depressed because I couldn't find brothers and sisters who fully followed the footsteps of Christ. I even began to condemn myself for not making the Christian life more attractive in my sermons.

I was finally cured of this when I moved closer to Christ myself. It did not improve the spiritual condition of those around me, but it did rid me of self-righteousness. I had particularly had trouble with a close friend named Tom. We lunched together often at a neighborhood deli. Tom and I loved talking about matters of faith and openly spoke together of our obligation to the cross. But no matter how much we spoke of the love of Christ, Tom never seemed to reach for the check when the waiter brought it to our table. I know it was a small thing, but my irritation grew each time I bought his meal. "God," I prayed, "help Tom to see that it is a rich testimony to Christ to pay one's own way in life." My heart soon began to grow as closed toward Tom as his wallet was toward me.

Only at the table in the wilderness did I begin to see how frequently I had drawn from the riches of Christ and repaid Him with a stingy obedience. Tom still isn't very generous, but I have learned to furnish his feast with greater cheer. At the table I have learned that he and I both are unfinished.

Ask God how you can minister to some other "unfinished saints" this week. Below list some specific actions that come out of your time of prayer.

____

____

____

____

Day 5 THE CHRIST WHO IS SUFFICIENT FOR US

You brought me out of the womb; you made me trust in you even at my mother's breast. From birth I was cast upon you; from my mother's womb you have been my God. Do not be far from me, for trouble is near and there is no one to help.—Psalm 22:9-11

In these verses the psalmist comes full circle. The Lord is ever sufficient—even in the midst of our troubles. Maturity in Christ allows us to reach the place where the despairing psalmist finally arrives. There we too may learn Christ's sufficiency.

The glory of all our shortcomings is that God is able to make up the difference between what we need and what we have: "My God will supply all your needs according to His riches in glory in Christ Jesus" (Phil. 4:19).

What do you think of the idea that God makes even our shortcomings glorify Himself?

- ❑ What an awesome God!
- ❑ Good, that excuses my sins.
- ❑ I don't believe anything but bad can come from sin.
- ❑ I don't understand how our shortcomings can glorify God.
- ❑ Other______________________________

Paraphrase what the apostle Paul said about his weakness in 2 Corinthians 12:9.

____

____

I have no need to be anxious, since God is a sparrow lover: "Aren't two sparrows sold for a penny? Yet not one of them falls to the ground without your Father's consent. ... Don't be afraid therefore; you are worth more than many sparrows" (Matt. 10:29,31).

His sufficiency in my troubled world is always adequate, no matter the dimensions of my need. When my infant son was taken with pneumonia, I saw him lying in a makeshift oxygen tent. I was terrified he might be taken from me. My fear grew larger and larger, until it camped like a wall of demons between me and Christ. It all but erased the face of my Host.

Describe a time when fear grew larger and "camped like a wall of demons" between you or someone you love and Christ.

____

____

____

____

Thinking back on that time, what lessons has Christ taught you through the process?

____

____

____

____

Mercifully, God's word came to me in power in the midst of my circumstance, and I yielded up my fear: "When I am afraid, I will trust in you" (Ps. 56:3). His sufficiency taught me to trust. My son recovered.

I find that all-surpassing sufficiency of which Giles Fletcher wrote:

He is a path, if any be misled,
He is a robe, if any naked be,
If any chance to hunger, He is bread,
If any be a bondman, He is free,
If any be but weak, how strong is He,
To dead men life He is, to sick men health,
To blind men sight, and to the needy wealth,
A pleasure without loss, a treasure without stealth.[6]

Which of Fletcher's metaphors for God mean the most to you and why?

____

____

____

____

Christ's sufficiency can be discovered only by those who confess their insufficiency. Driven before our confessed weakness, we at last arrive at the oracle of God's power and beg for His strength.

According to the previous paragraph, to what good purpose does God put failure and even our sin?

____

____

We can learn so much from Jesus at the wilderness table. Oh, that the psalmist might have known Jesus' compassion. At Christ's table, His love and power focus on our desperation. We learn His dependability. No matter when we flee to the table, we may be sure He will be there.

But the greatest benefit of this table of inwardness is that we learn about Christ's oneness with His Father. At the table, we clearly see that He and the Father are inseparable. Just as Jesus never walked alone, so He never comes to the table alone. And His trust in His Father is a model of how we are to trust Christ. Even the hell of Golgotha could not break His loyalty to His Father. In the same way, we are bonded to Christ.

Now we know the secret of both holiness and strength. We too have an enduring relationship with Jesus' Father. We are not orphans in this universe. The Father of Christ is our Father too, and He walks with us through the shadow of death, though hell should break loose around us.

This glory is ours: Through the valley we see the distant gleam of the trophy Christ has won. We are one with Him. Our union is the prize!

Spend some time with Christ at the wilderness table. Meet and talk with Him. And don't forget to listen. Below note anything you want to save from that time with Him.

____

____

____

____

____

____

____

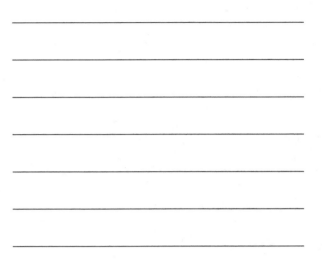

[1]Sergei Kourdakov, *The Persecutor* (Old Tappan, NJ: Fleming H. Revell, Spire Books, 1973), 219, 247, quoted in Tom Sine, *The Mustard Seed Conspiracy* (Waco, TX: Word, 1981), 196.

[2]Dorothy Sayers, quoted in Philip Yancey, *Open Windows* (Westchester, IL: Crossway, 1982), 79.

[3]William Shakespeare, *Macbeth*, act 5, scene 5, lines 24ff.

[4]Virginia Stem Owens, *And the Trees Clap Their Hands* (Grand Rapids, MI: Eerdmans, 1983), 55–56.

[5]Paul E. Billheimer, *Don't Waste Your Sorrows* (Ft. Washington, PA: Christian Literature Crusade, 1977), 82–83.

[6]Giles Fletcher, "He Is," in Phyllis Hobe, ed., *Dawnings: Finding God's Light in the Darkness* (Waco, TX: Word, 1981), 24.

WEEK 5

THE HOLY COMMUNION OF PRAYER

Day 1 PRAYER, A PASSION FOR GOD

As the deer pants for streams of water, so my soul pants for you, O God. My soul thirsts for God, for the living God. When can I go and meet with God?

—Psalm 42:1-2

The table in the wilderness holds but one loaf. Just as there is one Lord, one faith, one baptism, so is the bread of the table one communion. But this oneness is born of two hungers: We hunger for Christ; Christ longs for us. The church may create a desire for His fellowship, but its very rituals, public and busy as they are, often overwhelm and obscure the leisurely pace of His glorious table.

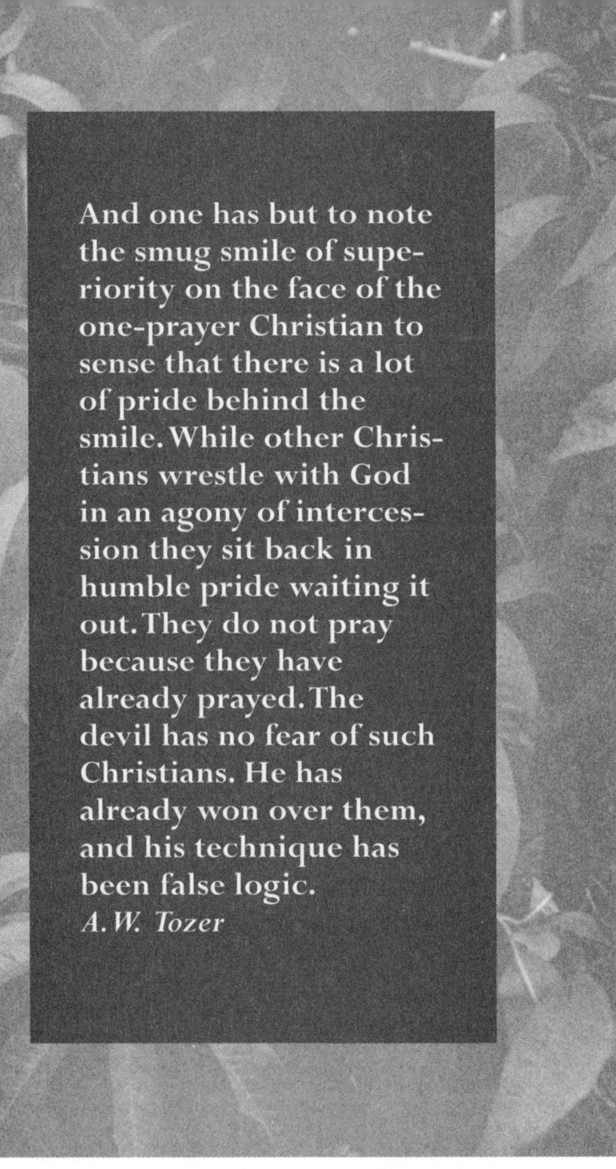

And one has but to note the smug smile of superiority on the face of the one-prayer Christian to sense that there is a lot of pride behind the smile. While other Christians wrestle with God in an agony of intercession they sit back in humble pride waiting it out. They do not pray because they have already prayed. The devil has no fear of such Christians. He has already won over them, and his technique has been false logic.
A. W. Tozer

Take time to slowly and meditatively read Psalm 42. With which thoughts of David do you most identify in the Psalm?

____

____

____

The writer of Psalm 42 articulates our passionate thirst for Christ. A deer victimized by the hunt could be driven to near madness. In the arid climate of ancient Palestine, water was scant. So the poor animal would fly ahead of her stalkers until she was forced to stop and take a drink. This stop could be her undoing. The psalmist likens our spiritual passion to this thirst-crazed deer. "When can I go and meet with God?" laments the poet. His hunger for intimacy must find satisfaction. He must find God, and he must find him now.

When have you been desperately hungry for God?

- ❑ following a time of tragedy in my life
- ❑ during a time of doubt and questioning
- ❑ when God had just done a work in my life
- ❑ when I had a need that only God could meet
- ❑ other ______________________________

Churchmanship alone will never sate our hunger for moments alone with our Host. Our longing hearts not only seek but also desire to remain at the wilderness table of Psalm 23.

I find my church involvement to be:

- ❑ more of a help than a hindrance to my personal communion with Christ.
- ❑ more of a hindrance than a help to my personal communion with Christ.
- ❑ sometimes a help, sometimes a hindrance to fellowship with Jesus.
- ❑ more of a hindrance than it used to be.
- ❑ less of a hindrance than it used to be.

How do you think a person can balance busyness and time alone with God?

____

____

The intimacy the psalmist thirsted for can be found only through a passion for God born of prayer. To achieve the intimacy of true oneness with Christ through prayer is to know true spirituality.

As author Donald Bloesch wrote, "The key to true piety is not to subscribe to the ethical teachings of Moses or of Jesus, nor is it to have the right ideas about God and reality. Instead it is being united with Christ by faith, then living the kind of life that proceeds from that union."[1] We are not to fear this intimacy, for the union comes as a product of the cross itself. Nothing except our reluctance prevents us from enjoying the intimacy of this union. The dividing wall has been broken down, and we are free to seek our fill of God's presence (see Eph. 2:14).

Fill in the blanks from the paragraph above:
Spiritual thirst comes from an intimacy found only

through a ________________ for God born of

________________.

If the you considered the stool shown below to represent the Christian faith. Paraphrase the words of Donald Bloesch by writing in the blanks the three parts of the faith.

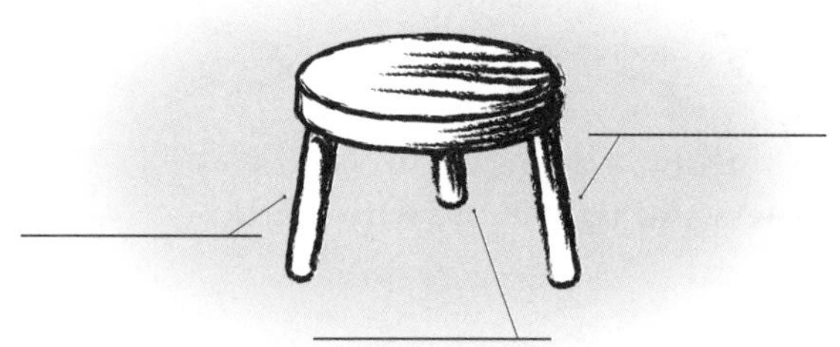

Which of the three parts do you tend to consider most important?

- ❑ adherence to ethical standards
- ❑ believing the right things
- ❑ a conscious union with Christ

What paradox do you see in the fact that a passion for God must be born of prayer?

____

____

____

The stool illustrates something key about the faith. Take away any one leg and the stool falls. Its occupant takes a tumble. However, ethics and beliefs don't bring life. Only union with Christ brings vitality to a person's walk, but dynamic union with Christ comes from time spent with Him. Passion for prayer comes only by praying. The paradox is that we must practice prayer to develop a passion for prayer.

Protestants have often left talk of union with Christ to Catholic mystics. Perhaps pursuing this union does not seem a worthy goal for our bottom-line, accomplishment mentality. A hunger for the inner life seems unproductive in a mega-church world. It does not seem to bring souls to the altar or provide a framework on which we may hang the ambitious programs of the church or denomination. Some may actually be suspicious of a oneness with Christ so absorbing that people might fail to keep the congregational machinery whirring. How sad!

Machines do not make a kingdom. A king does. At the center of true Christianity lies communion with a King. This communion, whatever we call it, is simply prayer. But it is fervent, ardent prayer. It is passion of desire. It is the thirst of a deer panting after water.

How would you answer the person who said that service in church is more important than spiritual union?

____

____

____

____

Prayer itself is not hard, but the will to pray is. We choose to have other kinds of conversations—so many, in fact, that we scarcely have a moment of silence. A pastor of my acquaintance puts it honestly:

> *I find it easier to* ***preach*** *on prayer than to* ***pray.***
> *I find it easier to* ***write*** *on prayer than to* ***pray.***
> *I find it easier to* ***talk*** *about Jesus than to* ***pray.***
> *I find* ***anything*** *I do in my Christian life easier than* ***praying!***[2]

When we talk about prayer, we leave the impression that we are people of prayer. But talking about prayer is only chitchat. We are not people of prayer until we pray. And we will never know spiritual intimacy until, like the psalmist, we thirst as a hunted deer.

End your day's study with a time of prayer. Do what you need to do to shut out the world. Go for a walk or into your closet. Beg the Father for a greater passion for Him.

Day 2 PRAYING WHEN GOD IS HARD TO FIND

My tears have been my food day and night, while

men say to me all day long, "Where is your God?"

—Psalm 42:3

God is sometimes hard to find. We call out to Him, but He eludes us. "Oh that I knew where I might find him," Job lamented (Job 23:3, KJV). Our passion for intimacy gets frustrated when we seek Him but can't find Him. Yet even when we can't find Him, we must seek Him again and again.

Why do you think a loving God would allow times when we seem unable to reach Him?

____

____

If you have gone through such a time and come out the other side, what treasures did you find in the darkness?

____

____

____

____

In Luke 18:1–8, Jesus told of a widow who repeatedly sought justice from a particular judge. Most of us are like that widow—intercession is the most common type of prayer for most Christians. We ask God to meet our needs. Jesus concludes that if an unrighteous judge will answer relentless requests, how much more will God, the righteous judge, respond to His people?

What complementary message do you find in Hebrews 4:16?

- ❑ Persistence in prayer pays big dividends.
- ❑ We can approach God confidently.
- ❑ God must answer our demands.
- ❑ Faith always gets results.

The widow was not arrogant. She was simply persistent. She believed the judge could be depended on to help. She sounds like she had been reading Hebrews 4. She would not let go of that confidence. But just as important as the judge's willingness to help was his ability to help. The widow believed in both. If our prayers lack confidence, it may be because we think God is too small to handle the immense petitions we bring Him or that He is not really concerned about us.

Some people teach that prayer is the key to receiving anything we want. We only need to "name it and claim it" by faith. If we are sick or poor, it is only because we have not prayed in faith. Such Christians quote Matthew 18:19: "If two of you on earth agree about any matter that you pray for, it will be done for you by My Father in heaven" or Matthew 21:22: "And everything—whatever you ask in prayer, believing—you will receive."

Are we not more prone to love the answer rather than the Answerer?

The idea that prayer ought to accomplish specific results seems prevalent among Christians in the West. At first glance, this type of prayer seems to be the kind of petition the widow used to get what she needed from the judge. But let us be honest about the parable. Do judges always answer persistent widows? Does persistent intercession always change things on our behalf? Is it always true that we "reap a harvest if we do not give up" (Gal. 6:9)?

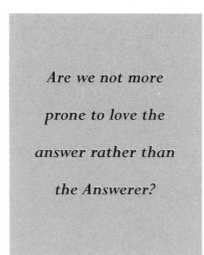

In contrast to the persistent widow, the psalmist found his petitions rising to heavens of brass. The doors of God's compassion were sealed against him. We cry like the psalmist: "Hey God, it's me! I'm bleeding! Where are you?"

Paul Billheimer, a noble heart in search of God, once asked:

> But HOW can the apparent failure [of God] be explained? A few are healed but the multitudes are not. A few have miraculous answers to prayer for healing and prosperity, but most do not. Are all those in this category to give up and wallow in self-pity and defeat? Is one to conclude that the multitudes who are not healed or delivered from grinding poverty must settle for second-class citizenship in the kingdom? Must the one who is not healed suffer with a sense of spiritual inferiority and the disappointing suspicion that we can have only God's second-best while a select minority who are healed and blessed with affluence pass as "God's chosen few"? Or is it possible for the great majority who remain financially limited or physically afflicted to make as great a contribution to the kingdom and bring as much joy to the heart of God and win as great an eternal reward as those who are favored with supernatural deliverance here and now?[3]

And worst of all, might not the "answer" obscure God rather than illuminate Him? Are we not more prone to love the answer rather than the Answerer?

Summarize today's lesson by describing how you would respond to the person who says God must give us what we desire in response to our prayer.

Day 3 THE DOWNCAST SOUL

These things I remember as I pour out my soul: how I used to go with the multitude, leading the procession to the house of God, with shouts of joy and thanksgiving among the festive throng. Why are you downcast, O my soul? Why so disturbed within me? Put your hope in God, for I will yet praise him, my Savior and my God. My soul is downcast within me; therefore I will remember you from the land of the Jordan, the heights of Hermon—from Mount Mizar.—Psalm 42:4-6

Railing at God for seeming to ignore our prayer may derive from our selfishness. Much of the time, when God seems deaf to our pleas, we have stormed the gates of heaven in a snit of self-interest. Our crisis intercession usually rises from our deep concern for ourselves. When we are frightened by death or duress, all of our best attempts to focus on the adequacy of God run aground.

Read the following illustration and then write a moral to the story.

> Many times during World War II, when Helmut Thielicke, the pastor of Stuttgart, was in the bomb shelters, he heard people from his congregation praying, "Lord, save us from the bombs." But their focus was on the attack and not on God. Even as they prayed, they did not picture God, but the bombs that were hurtling down upon them.

The moral to the story: ______________________

Ego can become a bully in intercession, making strong demands of heaven and pushing God around. But ego's worst fault may be that it sulks in a dour mood when it doesn't get its way. We become like the little boy who, just after his geography test, prayed earnestly, "Dear God, please let St. Louis be the capital of Missouri." Never mind that St. Louis has never been the capitol of Missouri. We must have what we ask. The boy's prayer may be earnest, but his ego is declaring its own desperate need to be right by bullying God to drop His own agenda for the world in order to embrace the child's.

Praying for ourselves often puts God in a box and makes Him the captive of our narrow will and piety.

In prayer have you ever tried to "push God around"? ❑ yes ❑ no ❑ maybe

Do you tend to act more like God's—
❑ adviser or ❑ worshiper?

How would you distinguish between the two approaches to God?

an adviser would ______________________________

____

a worshiper would ______________________________

____

Notice how the psalmist at first recalls the days of his victorious prayer life. Now he laments that while he is in great need, God is remote. The psalmist is traveling between great highs and lows, between fervency and stale hunger.

I recently read of a Christian college professor whose baby was very sick. Several times the professor and his wife called on their friends to intercede for the child. The crisis intercession was aimed at restoring the child's health, but in a little while, the infant died.

The zealous professor and his friends continued in prayer, no longer for healing but for the resurrection of the baby. After three days, when the baby had not yet revived, the local authorities interrupted the prayer meeting and removed the dead child from the midst of the pitiful, grieving parents. The sorrowing couple were doing nothing more than "naming and claiming" what they desperately wanted for themselves.

Praying for ourselves often puts God in a box and makes Him the captive of our narrow will and piety. His overall plan, I believe, is not subject to alteration by our will, however earnestly we pray.

What shall we say then? Is intercession wrong altogether?

No, but the spirit of intercession must always include the last line of Christ's great prayer in Gethsemane: "Not My will, but Yours, be done" (Luke 22:42). For Jesus to ask for deliverance from the cross was normal and natural, but He knew His Father's final decision was larger than His own desire to escape the pain. The Father had, in the life and death of His Son, a great plan for redeeming the world through the meeting of Their two wills. When those wills met, any petition might have been asked. But the submission of the Son's desires to the Father's plan was evidence of Their oneness. When we read John 17, we see how Christ's union with His Father resulted in great prayers of intercession for His church.

Read John 17:1-10. What does Jesus seem to mean when He talks of "glorifying" His Father?

___

___

___

This kind of prayer is much more rare than crisis intercession. One of Mother Teresa's prayers offers us another illustration: "Father, I pray for these sisters whom you have chosen to serve you and belong to you; they are yours, and you gave them to me; you want me to lead them to you; you wish them to be an image of your Son, your own perfect image that men might believe that you have sent him; that seeing their works, men may acknowledge that Christ was sent by you."[4]

What phrase do you find in each of the following Scriptures: Jeremiah 16:21, Ezekiel 6:14, 28:24?

___

___

Constantly Mother Teresa prayed that Christ would be formed in those she served and to whom she ministered. Paul wrote to the Galatians: "My children, again I am in the pains of childbirth for you until Christ is formed in you" (Gal. 4:19). On what is this glorious request based? The desire for our own conformity to Christ. In all these examples the end result is the same—that people would know that God is the Lord.

How do we avoid the psalmist's highs and lows and achieve a victorious evenness in our prayers? Here is the threefold secret of intercession: First, we should feel complete freedom to ask a loving Father for the desires of our heart. Second, we must agree that what we want can be set aside to meet the demands of a higher will. Third, our ultimate motivation for prayer should not be that we want something from God but that we want God.

Write in your own words the three principles for intercessory prayer.

1. ___

2. ___

3. ___

Take a recent subject for which you have prayed intercessory prayers and reword your prayer based on these principles

1. ___

___

2. ___

___

3. ___

___

Let me conclude today's study with a note on the glory of honest, conversational intercession. The strength of this kind of prayer is spontaneity. In his journal, John Wesley tells ecstatically of the time he first began to pray extemporaneously. As a high churchman, he had traditionally used liturgical forms. He was so taken with the joy of spontaneous communication that he pledged never to pray rote prayers again. The mystics often used structured communication when they approached Christ; but rote prayers, having been learned by heart, can cease to be a stimulus to the imagination.

What could you do to improve the quality of your communication with God?

❑ become more spontaneous rather than repeating learned prayers
❑ practice being more genuine rather than using the same words
❑ work on my language to communicate in fresh terms
❑ learn to be more expressive of my emotions in prayer
❑ seek to be more honest in pouring out the concerns of my heart
❑ be less self-focused by praying more for God's pleasure and for the needs of others

❑ other actions I could take ____________________

____

____

____

The psalmist cries, "These things I remember as I pour out my soul" (Ps. 42:4) From the psalmist's imagination had come the image of a deer panting for water. From his imagination grew the picture of a towering, invisible force that would at last focus its strength on his weakness. Faith grows by leaps and bounds when our imagination joins forces with holiness.

Godly imagination must, however, constantly run on a new track, or it will, in time, become lifeless. A living imagination is essential to prayer. When we close our eyes to shut out the seen world, the images of an unseen world emerge. My own imagination ever visualizes God, high and lifted up, stooping to my needs, giving me the Christ for whom I hunger. Like Wesley, I rarely pray rote prayers. While it may not be to my credit, I do not actually know very many of them. I find Christ anew in every prayer.

When the words and images are new, the possibilities and the hope also are new. Through conversational intercession we may approach the Father to ask for things. Christ, deeply in love with us, may say no. Yet whatever His answer, we love Him because He is Christ and not because He grants our petitions.

Day 4 DEEP CALLING TO DEEP

Deep calls to deep in the roar of your waterfalls;

all your waves and breakers have swept over me.

—Psalm 42:7

When "deep calls to deep," we echo the passion of the thirsty deer. We are no longer content with shallow prayer. We want to move into a more satisfying, more intimate walk with God.

How can we join the psalmist's deep-to-deep pursuit of spiritual unity with God? What hinders us is our basic failure to pray for this intimacy, and that is the direct result of a breakdown in our relationship with Him. Our failure is not because we don't love prayer but because we do not love Christ.

"Oh," we exclaim, "if we'd lived in His day,
if we could've heard
and seen
and touched Him,

how dearly we'd have loved Him,
how gladly we'd have left everything to follow Him!"

Really?
Haven't we ever seen or touched Him?
We can commune with Him every day.[5]

A devoted husband doesn't say, "I love talking to my wife." He says, "I love my wife." Theresa confessed that when she first joined the Carmelites, she prayed that God would make her pray for hours every day, as though much rigorous prayer was the quintessence of devotion. God gave her no such schedule. What He did was give her an appetite for Himself, and once her hunger for God was whetted, she prayed without ceasing. God does not order hungry birds to eat, nor thirsty beasts to drink. Hunger itself seeks food, as thirst seeks water.

Our failure is not because we don't love prayer but because we do not love Christ.

Circle the greatest form of devotion:

hours of prayer every day	to love Christ passionately

Alone with our Host, we find the delight Theresa found in her interior castle or that John of the Cross found in his "spouse." We will pursue our love through a joyous, inner intimacy. In the power of that union, we will constantly walk in joy with our Host.

Brother Lawrence, near the end of his life, reminded us that this gracious, delightful, and continuing joy is not always derived from formal worship:

It is not necessary for being with God to be always at church. We may make an oratory of our heart wherein to retire from time to time to converse with Him in meekness, humility, and love. Every one is capable of such familiar conversation with God, some more, some less. He knows what we can do. Let us begin, then. Perhaps He expects but one generous resolution on our part. Have courage. We have but little time to live; you are near sixty-four, and I am almost eighty. Let us live and die with God. Sufferings will be sweet and pleasant to us while we are with Him; and the greatest pleasures will be, without Him, a cruel punishment to us. May He be blessed for all. Amen.[6]

Brother Lawrence had found the blessing of a constant companionship with the Son of God. We do not achieve a blending of our spirit with God's, as in some chummy relationship. Rather, we participate in His greatness. Some kneel and cry out. They weep and laugh hysterically, believing that God is thrumming the emotional strings of their nervous systems. When God moves in fullness into our lives, the riches of His glory certainly can be expected to awaken our emotional responses. Yet the key is not the emotional evidence of His indwelling but the indwelling itself. The better we know Him, the more we will honor Him.

Which description more nearly fits your natural response to emotionalism?

- ❑ quiet and reserved
- ❑ open and transparent
- ❑ stoic
- ❑ overflowing with emotion

How do you feel about displays of emotion?

____

____

Emotionalism often fuels large rallies. But as when sexual intimacy is opened to a group, it at once becomes obscene, so mass spiritual intimacy fosters a similar obscenity. The danger of ecstatic utterances in large groups is that mere emotion may be substituted for true union with the Holy.

Yet we often tremble before all thoughts of union with the Spirit. Intimacy with the Holy terrifies us. But the silence of the wilderness table absorbs our fear, and we are enveloped in oneness. Then deep does indeed call to deep, and the intimacy of the table sets the tone of our union with Christ.

How can you foster greater depth in your relationship to God?

____

____

____

____

____

Day 5 LISTENING PRAYER

By day the LORD directs his love, at night his song is with me—a prayer to the God of my life.

—Psalm 42:8

"His song is with me" indicates that the psalmist is learning the most valuable part of prayer: listening! That listening is such an important part of prayer should not surprise us. Listening is exactly half of every conversation.

Communication is two-way. God's words should comprise fully half of our prayers. Eastern mystics offer an odd riddle: "What is the sound of one hand clapping?" We might as well ask, "What is meaningful communication with only one voice?"

God is not just an ear. He is also a voice. If He never speaks, is it safe to assume that He ever listens? A mute God is soon absent. The listening prayer is a prayer of relationship. Our listening invites our silence, a shouting silence, but silence nonetheless. The psalmist sees God's part of the prayer as a song—a song to which he must listen.

One major barrier to the listening prayer is focus. The mind is a busy thoroughfare, bearing all kinds of vehicles—each honking to make headway. Earlier I wrote about the emptying process, kenotic meditation. This stops the chatter so we can converse with God in the silence. It cannot be done in a few minutes a day. It occupies a life. Here, in the patient silence, our humanity becomes more human. Here the image of God in us becomes a clearer mirror of the Spirit. Our being is united with the source of all being.

What kinds of "chatter" do you have to deal with most on the thoroughfare of your mind? Rate the top distractions for you.

____ Busyness: I find myself thinking of all I need to do.
____ Guilt: I feel unworthy to be in Christ's presence.
____ Self-centeredness: I'm more obsessed with my needs than His presence.
____ Unbelief: I find myself doubting God's existence and interest.
____ Low Self-image: I can't imagine that God would bother with me.
____ Other ____________________________

In listening, God resolves our inner contradictions. He unravels our tangled psychology. Listening for God in our devotion keeps Him from being a mute deity. The great saint of the inner life, Frank Laubach, once saw an enormous dam, complete with turbines and electrical gear—but not a single light bulb was being lit. When he asked why the turbines weren't rotating, he was told that the valve was closed. The Almighty wants us to be open to Him. Our silence is a door for Him to enter. Our silence is an ear for us to hear. The psalmist is right. The music of God is all around us. We must learn to listen.

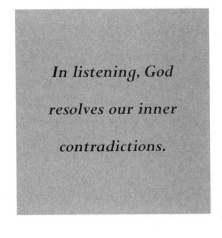

In listening, God resolves our inner contradictions.

Beside Laubach's image of silence as the valve draw or describe your own analogy for silence as the entry point for God's power:

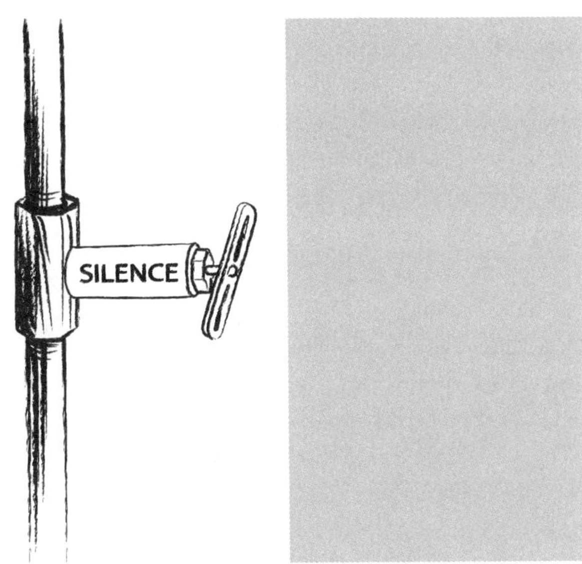

Madame Guyon, the French mystic, once thought that liturgical praying was enough for her spiritual life. Soon she realized that prayer was a conversation between two. Only then did she experience real union with God

Read Madame Guyon's statements below and circle the benefits that result from personal rather than formalistic prayer.

O my God, if the value of prayer were but known, the great advantage which accrues to the soul from conversing with Thee, and what consequence it is of to salvation, everyone would be assiduous in it. It is a stronghold into which the enemy cannot enter. He may attack it, besiege it, make a noise about its walls; but while we are faithful and hold our station, he cannot hurt us...

The only way to Heaven is prayer; a prayer of the heart, which every one is capable of, and not of reasonings which are the fruits of study, or exercise of the imagination, which, in filling the mind with wandering objects, rarely settle it; instead of warming the heart with love to God, they leave it cold and languishing. Let the poor come, let the ignorant and carnal come; let the children without reason or knowledge come, let the dull or hard hearts which can retain nothing come to the practice of prayer and they shall become wise.[7]

Throughout the Scriptures one phrase pounds like a jackhammer: "The Lord said." It is amazing that we are not utterly jolted to a standstill by its frequency! The Lord speaks, and those who serve Him listen. The Bible itself issues out of the reality of the God who speaks.

All of us have known times when it seemed as though God were not listening. The exact opposite is true. The more urgent our intercession, the more raucously our necessity roars, leaving God seemingly mute. At times, grief can scream at such a pitch that God seems silent. But He is not. Like any loving parent, He reaches out for His children when they hurt. Yet hurting children are often too involved in their pain to see beyond it.

Rewrite the following concept in your own words: "Intercession frenzied by need circumvents what it seeks to establish: an audience with God."

____

____

____

____

Like people who are drowning, our cries for help prevent us from hearing the one who will save us. I am intrigued by the truth of these raucous lines of doggerel:

We mutter and sputter
We fume and we spurt.
We mumble and grumble;
Our feelings get hurt.
We can't understand things.
Our vision grows dim,
When all that we need
Is a moment with him.[8]

A dear woman in our congregation was diagnosed with terminal cancer and began praying for God to heal her. She was earnest and in great need. God was reaching out to her, but the pain of her cancer clamored so loudly that she could not see or hear Him. In the weeks just before her death, we focused less and less on the crisis. We began to meet for Scripture reading and the prayer of listening. God did not choose to heal her, but we did discover that God was listening; and the woman learned to listen too. Her listening did not cure her, but in a real sense it healed her. And even as the cancer grew, so did her inner peace.

Listening in prayer sanctifies our entire world. Anthropologist Teilhard de Chardin said, "Nothing here below is profane for those who know how to see. On the contrary everything is sacred."[9] Teilhard is right, yet Romans 10:17 says that faith comes not by seeing but by hearing. For me it is better to say, "Nothing here in this world is profane for those who know how to hear."

Nature may serve as the best closet of prayer. Under the broad canopy of sky, we may discover the fortress of the Holy. Here, in the overwhelming sanctuary of the wide outdoors, God speaks loudly. Here He uses all He has made like a megaphone. His gracious tones reverberate from moon and stars, from rocks and hills and streams.

Yahweh is the Hebrew covenant name for God. It seems to have originated in the idea of "the god of storms." (It is a "breathy" word that may have its origin in the sound of wind.) Yahweh—the desert wind, alive with the stinging, peppering sand that roars over caravans and shepherds' tents. Yahweh called to Job from the whirlwind and said, "Where were you when I laid the earth's foundation? Tell me, if you understand. Who marked off its dimensions? Surely you know! Who stretched a measuring line across it? On what were its footings set, or who laid its cornerstone—while the morning stars sang together and all the angels shouted for joy?" (Job 38:4-7). Here the Maker speaks in the immensity of that which He made, but only to those who are listening.

When does a song become a prayer? When we get the Christ-view of that song. To get the Christ-view is what I call "Christifying" the world around us. No word adequately describes how praying believers view the world in which they walk. Christifying is consciously viewing the people and circumstances in our lives through the eyes of Christ. Ordinary events become cosmic when seen this way. Even people's ordinariness explodes with meaning as we see their potential salvation and service to the holy Christ. In Christifying, the whole world will shout to us of the reality of God. The poet

Francis Thompson said he could not even pick a flower without causing an inner trembling in the distant stars.

Try your own exercise in "Christifying." Pick someone you know or that you have just seen. Without identifying the particular person, list as many aspects of the person's value and purpose to Christ. (Plan to share your list with your group).

____

____

____

____

____

____

____

____

I love sitting in an airport terminal and watching those who scurry by, unaware of the Christ who smiles and waits to show them His gracious love. At such moments I see that there is an unknown God (Acts 17:23) who needs declaring but who, even before He is declared to the inattentive, sees and loves them and yearns to redeem them.

I generally think of Christifying my world as painting the face of the Savior on the anxious, hurried faces about me. As soon as they are autographed with His name, they yield to meaning and to real life.

Inwardness, communion with the Holy, is found in prayer—listening prayer—and in Christifying our world. Each night, we should examine our lives:

Did I thirst for God as a deer thirsts for water?
Did I talk to God today?
Yes, and more than talk, I listened.
Did I listen? Did I see Christ in my world?
Yes, I saw nothing but Christ.

If these are our answers, we have truly prayed without ceasing. Listening is prayer. It is the formidable silence we give to God so He can be heard and can take part in our lives. Only then can we enter into union with the Holy. In such listening we find a companion at the lonely table of Psalm 23 and dine on a meal of glory.

---

[1]Donald G. Bloesch, *Faith and Its Counterfeits* (Downers Grove, IL: InterVarsity Press, 1981), 19.

[2]Jack Taylor, "Prayer...The Priority!" in Ralph W. Neighbour Jr., comp., *Future Church* (Nashville, TN: Broadman, 1980), 79.

[3]Paul E. Billheimer, *Don't Waste Your Sorrows* (Ft. Washington, PA: Christian Literature Crusade, 1977), 21.

[4]Edward Le Joly, *Servant of Love* (San Francisco: Harper and Row, 1977), 35.

[5]Louis Evely, *That Man Is You,* trans. Edmond Bonin (New York: Paulist, 1963), 3.

[6]Brother Lawrence, *The Practice of the Presence of God* (Mt. Vernon, NY: Peter Pauper, 1963), 48.

[7]Madame Guyon, *Madame Guyon* (Chicago, IL: Moody Press), 41–42.

[8]Earl D. Radmacher, *You and Your Thoughts* (Palm Springs, CA: Ronald N. Haynes, 1982), 99.

[9]Teilhard de Chardin, quoted in Leo Buscaglia, *Personhood* (New York: Pawcett Columbine, 1982), 118.

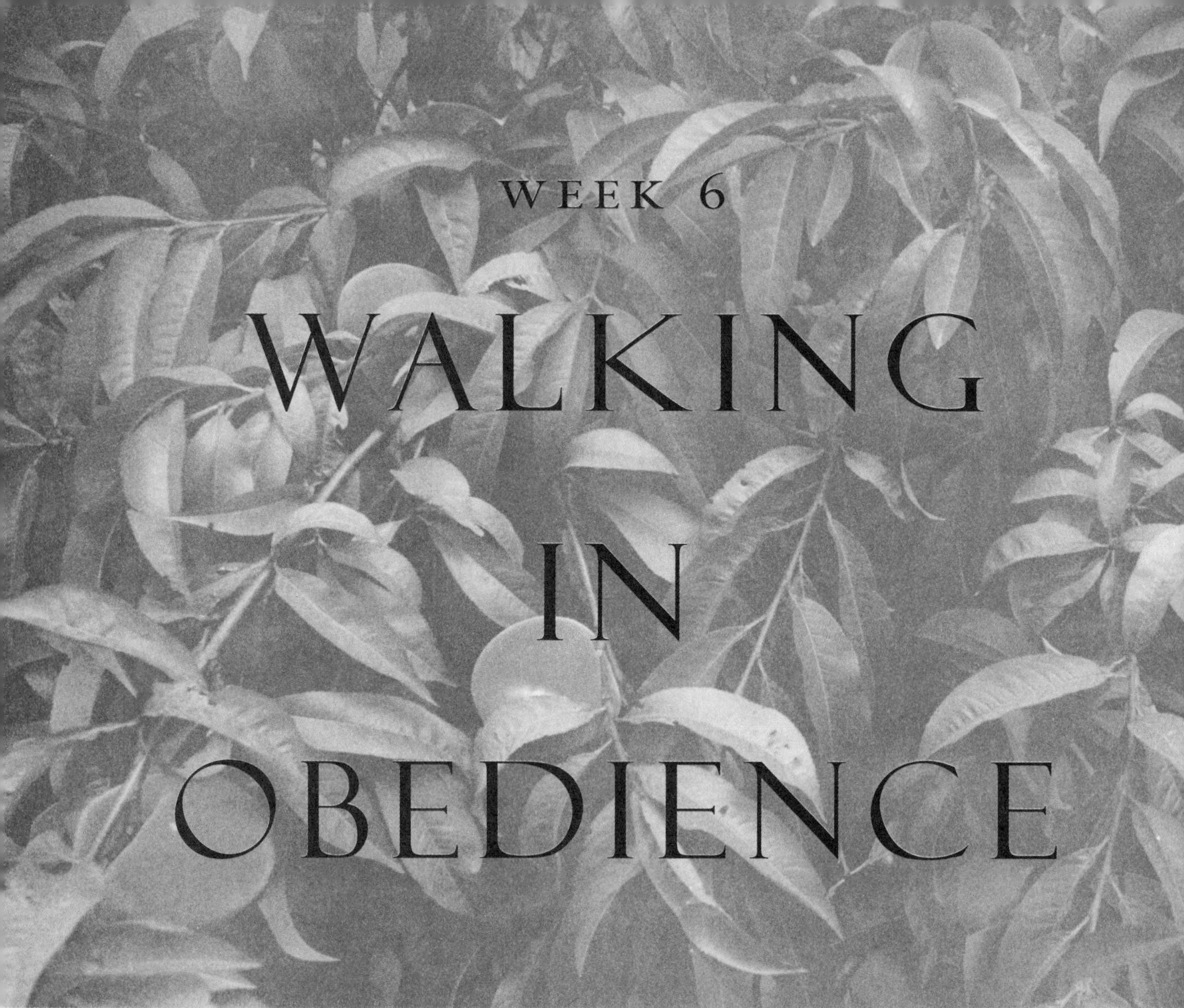

Day 1 WALKING IN OBEDIENCE

You are my portion, O Lord; I have promised to obey your words. I have sought your face with all my heart; be gracious to me according to your promise.

—Psalm 119:57–58

The most important word in the New Testament is *Lord.* It is a word we cannot say without implying our own surrender and obedience. Yet we use the word Lord loosely and inconsistently. Jesus, in noticing how glibly we use the word, asked, "Why do you call me 'Lord, Lord,' and don't do the things I say?" (Luke 6:46,). To obey is to call Christ Lord; to disobey is to claim the word for ourselves. The issue of all disciples, therefore, is whether they shall have a lord or be one.

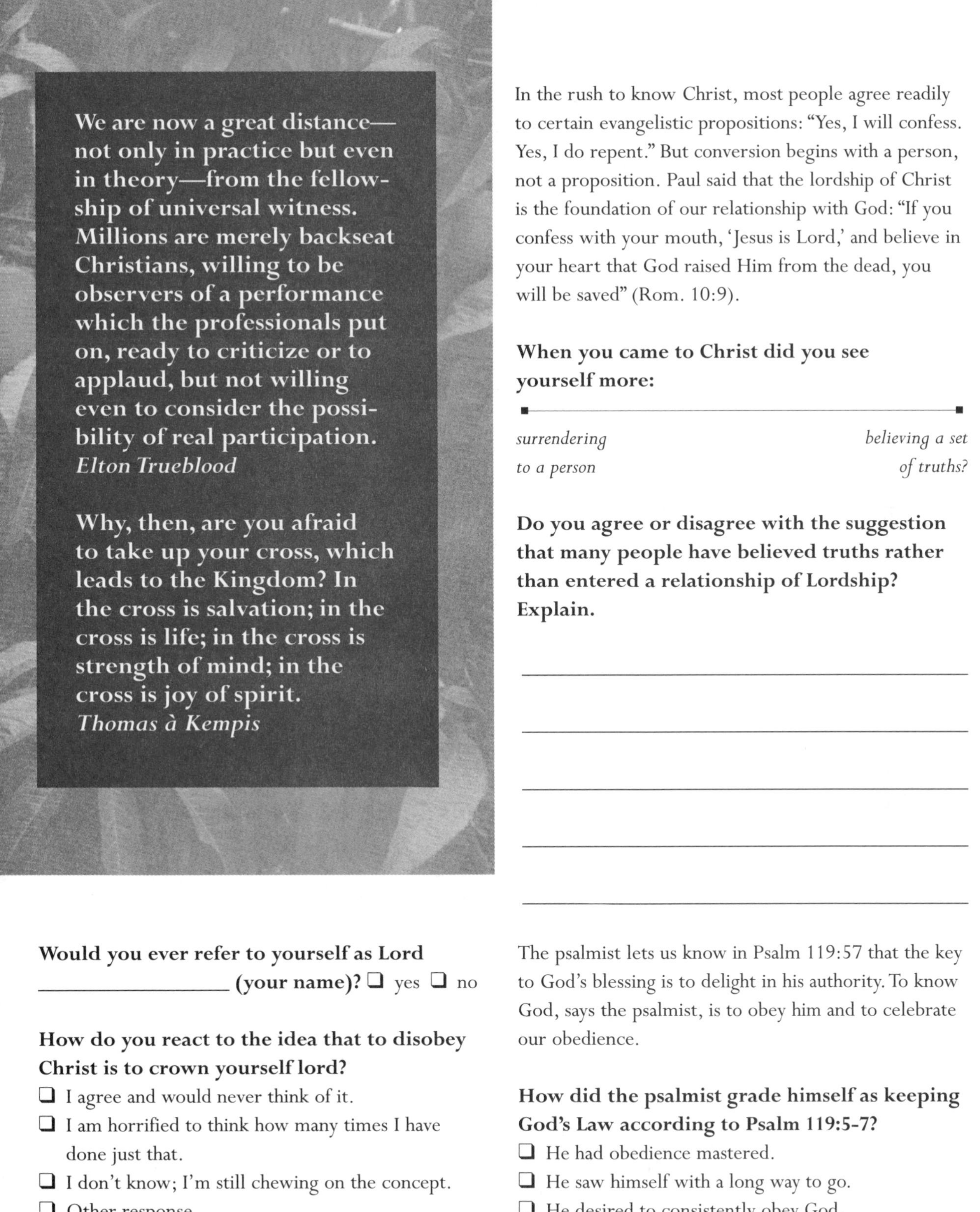

We are now a great distance—not only in practice but even in theory—from the fellowship of universal witness. Millions are merely backseat Christians, willing to be observers of a performance which the professionals put on, ready to criticize or to applaud, but not willing even to consider the possibility of real participation.
Elton Trueblood
Why, then, are you afraid to take up your cross, which leads to the Kingdom? In the cross is salvation; in the cross is life; in the cross is strength of mind; in the cross is joy of spirit.
Thomas à Kempis

In the rush to know Christ, most people agree readily to certain evangelistic propositions: "Yes, I will confess. Yes, I do repent." But conversion begins with a person, not a proposition. Paul said that the lordship of Christ is the foundation of our relationship with God: "If you confess with your mouth, 'Jesus is Lord,' and believe in your heart that God raised Him from the dead, you will be saved" (Rom. 10:9).

When you came to Christ did you see yourself more:

■————————————————■

surrendering to a person — *believing a set of truths?*

Do you agree or disagree with the suggestion that many people have believed truths rather than entered a relationship of Lordship? Explain.

____

____

____

____

____

Would you ever refer to yourself as Lord ________________ (your name)? ❑ yes ❑ no

How do you react to the idea that to disobey Christ is to crown yourself lord?

- ❑ I agree and would never think of it.
- ❑ I am horrified to think how many times I have done just that.
- ❑ I don't know; I'm still chewing on the concept.
- ❑ Other response ________________________

The psalmist lets us know in Psalm 119:57 that the key to God's blessing is to delight in his authority. To know God, says the psalmist, is to obey him and to celebrate our obedience.

How did the psalmist grade himself as keeping God's Law according to Psalm 119:5-7?

- ❑ He had obedience mastered.
- ❑ He saw himself with a long way to go.
- ❑ He desired to consistently obey God.

What was the psalmist's desire and goal (v. 7)?

How do you think your life would be different if you reached the place of genuinely delighting in God's authority?

In spite of the psalmist's mandate to obey, some people still say, "I accepted Christ as my Savior at a young age, but I did not accept him as my Lord until much later." This curious double-stepping into grace ignores the fact that the Christ who saves can only become our Lord as we submit to His sovereignty. Becoming a Christian without submitting ourselves to Christ is impossible.

Dietrich Bonhoeffer referred to all such ideas of lordless salvation as cheap grace. Theologian W. T. Conner put it this way: "Long ago I accepted Jesus as my Lord, thereby making it possible for him to be my Savior." So the psalmist is right to encourage us to delight in God's requirement so we can find joy in our obedience.

Personalize Psalm 119:33-34, and verse 165 by writing a prayer using and responding to the words of the verses.

Day 2 OBEDIENCE ABOVE ALL

Teach me, O Lord, to follow your decrees; then I will keep them to the end.—Psalm 119:33

The psalmist must be admired here, for he states one of the most important principles: When we sign the Lord's covenant of obedience, it is a lifelong contract. We must give all we are and have for as long as we live. The poet agrees that we must cherish God's decrees to the point that we "will keep them to the end." We have no right to claim a love for God if we walk the selfish ledges of disregard for what God requires of us.

List all the areas where you can honestly say Jesus is Lord of your life

Did you think of areas like time and money? What about life issues like relationships?

Shakespeare's *The Merchant of Venice* supplies a great picture of the kind of commitment Christ demands. In the play, Portia asks each of her three suitors to select the cask containing her picture. Her portrait is the lucky suitor's ticket to the marriage altar. The first of the three casks is gold. Across the top are the words, "Whoso chooseth me will gain what many men desire." The second cask is silver, and across the top of it is inscribed the phrase, "Whoso chooseth me shall get what he deserves." But Bassanio picks the lead cask with the formidable inscription, "Whoso chooseth me must give and hazard all he hath."[1] Beneath this demanding label lies Portia's picture and the invitation to a life of sacrifice and self-denial. Here is both the greatest challenge and the greatest reward. The lordship of Christ, likewise, comes beneath the inscription of the lead cask. It comes to the one who, like the psalmist, is willing to say, "I will follow my commitments to God; I will keep them to the end."

The lordship of Christ comes to the one who is willing to say, "I will follow my commitments to the end."

Think about the three inscriptions. Write what you think would be the end result in a person's character who followed each of the options:

gain what many men desire ______________________

____

get what he deserves __________________________

____

give and hazard all he has______________________

____

Did you note that getting what we desire often proves to be more curse than blessing? And does getting our wants met make us strong or weak? How about what we deserve? Where would you end up if you got exactly what you deserve? For myself I conclude that the third option may be more difficult but it clearly results in character development far greater than the other two.

Obedience implies submission. Submission seems applicable only to a servant, or better yet, a slave. The apostle Paul embraced this truth and the obedience to Christ that followed from such a relationship. In some of his letters, Paul calls himself a *doulos christou,* a slave of Christ. Submission is a distasteful word these days. We preach freedom and are threatened by every idea of constraint. But is being a slave to godly obedience the end of our liberty or the beginning?

How would you answer that last question?
❑ the beginning of liberty ❑ the end of liberty
Explain your answer.

____

____

____

____

Some years ago, Elisabeth Elliot wrote *The Liberty of Obedience*. This paradoxical title drew me to the book. I had not read far when I discovered that the title itself was the point of the book. God gives us liberty in direct proportion to our deliberate submission. In our submission to God's Son, the Spirit moves into us and becomes one with us. Mother Teresa closely identified with the Spirit and spent each day submitted to her Father in heaven. "There is no demand so unreasonable," she said, "that God cannot make it of my life."

How do you feel about making Mother Teresa's statement your own?

- ❑ I wholeheartedly embrace it. God can make any demand of me.
- ❑ I want to agree to it, but I fear God may ask of me more than I can give.
- ❑ I cannot honestly say I am that surrendered to God's demands.
- ❑ other________________________________

One couple I know served Christ in Argentina for thirty-five years. The home where they spent their retirement was modest but spiritually elegant. An aura of joy enveloped these saints, for they had been set free from any need to serve themselves. They did not horde the days for some agenda of their own. Their love for their Savior made obeying Him a delight. The more they served Christ, the greater their hunger to please Him. Pleasing God became their passion to the end of their days. None I have ever met were so free.

On a scale of 1 to 10, where 10 is totally free, how would you describe your freedom in Christ in each of the following areas. Freedom from …

fear	1	2	3	4	5	6	7	8	9	10
worry	1	2	3	4	5	6	7	8	9	10
greed	1	2	3	4	5	6	7	8	9	10
lust	1	2	3	4	5	6	7	8	9	10

What one thing could you begin to do today that would result in greater obedience to Christ and therefore greater freedom in Christ?

____

____

____

Day 3 DISCERNING OBEDIENCE

Give me understanding, and I will keep your law and obey it with all my heart. Direct me in the path of your commands, for there I find delight.

—Psalm 119:34–35

The psalmist is not just pleading for a heart of obedience; he is asking God how he is to spend his obedience in a broken world. He wants to know what his obedience means. He wants not only to obey God but to obey Him with understanding. When I was young, my mother wanted me to do well in school. I was bright enough to do "OK" without really applying myself. But I soon found myself doing better than simply "OK" because I knew my mother really wanted me to excel. Gradually I came to accept her will, not because I saw any long-term point in excellence but because I could see it brought her so much joy.

Across the years, I have noticed that those with extraordinary commitment are apt to be better leaders and thinkers than those who merely get by with "OK." The psalmist is eager to obey, but he wants insight on why the rigors of a real struggle are to be preferred to a more casual obedience. So he pleads for understanding in the matter.

Do you find obedience to a command easier if you know why you are asked to obey?

❑ yes ❑ no ❑ not sure

If so, why does understanding aid obedience?

____

____

____

How would you explain to your child the importance of rigorous rather than casual obedience to the commands of God?

____

____

____

____

I learned, by the time I left high school, that even if I could see no logic in the things my mother asked of me, it was worth obeying her just to see what a charge she got out of it. She always seemed so pleased when I did what she asked. In the course of time I became pleased with what I did because she was pleased.

One winter I was leading a student conference in Canada when I met the son of a prestigious physician. He was wearing a heavy and handsome winter coat. "Nice coat!" I said.

"Thank you," he replied.

In further discussion, I discovered that it had been purchased at a secondhand store for twenty-five cents. "Why did you buy a secondhand coat?" I asked the son, out of earshot of his famous father. "Your father is rich!"

"Because my father also buys secondhand coats," the young man answered.

I listened long enough to discover that the physician had re-evaluated his whole economic position and had led his sons in the same new direction. They honored the lordship of Christ by dressing in other people's castaways. They used the money they might have spent on new clothes to travel to third-world countries to practice medicine. Fettered to this great commitment, the doctor had yet liberated himself and his sons. Such freedom as they knew is only gained as we break our ties to our material ambitions and yield to the Savior.

In Mark 10:17-22, why did the young man end up sorrowful?

❑ a large Pharisee was standing on his foot
❑ Jesus demanded that he leave father and mother
❑ because he had great wealth

Were his possessions ultimately a blessing or a curse? Why?

____

____

____

The secret of disciplining children begins in the nursery. The best of discipline aims at breaking extreme self-will, but never the human spirit. The problem of self-will is that it usually wills all the wrong things. Nursery children sometimes crave what is bad for them. They may want to pick up a live charcoal from the hearth merely because the color is pleasing. We may warn them about this, but warning alone may not be enough to squelch their unwise desires.

Our relationship to Christ gives birth to a passion to obey Him. The more we love Him, the more we want Him to be part of our affairs.

The psalmist is a lover of his Lord and desires a continual preoccupation with God. Brother Lawrence called this hungering relationship the practice of the presence of God. This may also be what Paul meant when he spoke of praying without ceasing (1 Thess. 5:17). God promises power to all who walk with Christ in such continual preoccupation!

The highest kind of obedience never comes from constantly asking, "What will you have me do?" It is born in the moment-by-moment rehearsal of our love for Christ. My wife and I love each other, and as we live in the enjoyment of our relationship, we continually surrender our wills to each other. We do not continually ask, "What would you like me to do?" Because of our relationship, we know each other's desires, and we do all we can to meet them—often without any exchange of words.

On what does the question "What will you have me to do?" focus?

❑ God's desires
❑ my performance
❑ the needs of others

What is the focus of moment-by-moment rehearsal of our love for Christ?

❑ myself ❑ others ❑ Christ

Do you tend to focus more on—

❑ Christ ❑ your performance

When God's silence envelops us, though no words pass, the holy Presence himself communicates. He communicates the divine will and leaves our own desire empty and craving instruction.

Day 4 THE FOUNDATION WORD

Turn my heart toward your statutes and not toward selfish gain.—Psalm 119:36

The psalmist has grown enough in his walk with God that he craves a preoccupation with the requirements of God. He wants the Lord to turn his heart toward God's law. This is his ready acknowledgement that he is willing to enter into a lifetime of study, for the statutes of God cannot be mastered otherwise.

Do you tend to think of a lifetime of seriously studying God's Word as basic to discipleship? Why or why not?

____

____

____

____

What benefits do you think would come from having your heart turned toward God's law?

____

____

____

In my years as a professor, I have found only a few students who seem to catch the clear command of God that they have been called to a lifetime study of His Word. Most wish they could just absorb the difficult lessons of Scripture by osmosis. A few do step up to the plate. What is exciting about this is that these few students find themselves developing a real romance with scholarship. It's intoxicating, when we turn our lives toward God's statutes, and soon find that we are in love with learning.

But the psalmist doesn't want knowledge for knowledge's sake. He wants knowledge to help him bypass the selfish life. He wants to use what he is learning to make the world a better place, to enhance the presence of God in the world. His study exists to improve and redeem the fallen world.

Study is crucial, and it's hard work. We would rather rest or recreate. Study is a discipline that focuses on the glorious Word of God. This is to be understood in a double sense: both the written Word of God and the incarnate Word of God.

Psalm 119 is dedicated to God's written Word. But in Christ we go beyond the psalmist's love of the written Word to our sheer adoration of the incarnate Word—the *logos* of God. Why? Because the written Word reveals the living Word.

The written Word must be studied if we are to know the incarnate Word. Let us concentrate here on how the psalmist's longing for the written Word becomes at last the foundation of the inner life.

Knowing the Bible is not an option for those who want to know true inwardness. No one stays for long at the table of Psalm 23 who does not also study Scripture. Mystics without study are only spiritual romantics who want relationship without effort.

> ***Those who penned Scripture did not write in the peaceful calm of seminary chapels but in the hurriedness of dying empires.***

The best learning of Scripture is not done in a theology class or in the high towers of religious institutions. The psalmist learned his love of Scripture in the laboratory of life. The written Word of God came originally from the pens of forty writers over a period of fourteen hundred years. These people were sometimes caught in the snare of historic upheavals. They suffered martyrdom and endured the pressure of imprisonment and the horror of military sieges. They did not write in the peaceful calm of seminary chapels but in the hurriedness of dying empires. Likewise, their writings are meant to speak practically in the uncertain days of our lives. But these seasons of pain have their place in our obedience.

Why do you think the psalmist asked God to "turn [his] eyes away from worthless things"? (Ps. 119:37).

____

____

____

____

The psalmist saw fearing God as a state to be desired and as the end result of studying His Word. We must remember, as Jean-Pierre de Caussade wrote, that "the Holy Spirit is writing a living gospel with the pen of action, which we will only be able to read on the day of glory when, fresh from the presses of life, it will be published."[2]

I think the writer of Psalm 119 would have said, "I practice daily what I believe; everything else is religious talk." Only God's Word mixed in with life can make Scripture serve inwardness. For inwardness can never come at the price of withdrawing from our world. Bailey Smith, a noted Baptist pastor, put it this way:

> *Far too many people have used the Bible like a medical student uses a cadaver. They examine it, dissect it, perform surgery on it, familiarize themselves with it, and learn its distinctive qualities. But as that future doctor cannot give life to that dead piece of humanity, so these people never get the Word alive in their life. They somehow fail to remember that the people who hated Jesus most were biblical scholars and had Scriptures over their doorposts, strapped to their bodies, and quoted chapters of it when their narrow-minded interpretation supported their warped views.*[3]

Mark the following *true* or *false* based on the Bailey Smith quote above.

____ 1. Many people seek to know the Bible as an academic exercise.

____ 2. Knowing Scripture guarantees knowing God.

____ 3. If the people of Jesus' day had known the Scripture, they would have followed Christ.

____ 4. People sometimes use the Scripture instead of hearing from the God of the Scripture.

Scripture used only to fortify theology is quarrelsome.

Scripture used only to fortify theology is quarrelsome. Someone always wants to discuss the "discrepancies" in the Bible. Yet when reason seems at an end and life is desperate, we pick up the Scriptures to search not for discrepancies but for truth. I marked all but the third statement in the exercise true.

Certainly, in our devotion, we should not lose respect for biblical scholarship. The discipline of formal study makes the Scripture practical, and disciplined study correlates truth in ways that cement it all together. We come to the wilderness table mind first, ready to learn the written Word from the Word made flesh. Knowledge for knowledge's sake may end in disgrace, but when the laws of God appear to be most wholesome—utterly good—they concern themselves with how to help a sick world get well again.

Much of this can only happen when we leave the world, with all its pain, and get alone with God to seek how He wants us to begin our ministry. When we leave the table, we should have two different attitudes. First, we must sense God's own need to help the bleeding planet. If we don't spend time alone with God, we cannot feel what God feels about the pain in our world. Second, we must be willing to leave the intimate and wonderful place of prayer to enter into the world and to serve it by binding up its hurts and lifting its eyes toward God.

Jesus often took time to be alone to pray, but these times were always retreats. Between His periodic withdrawals, He touched and healed people. He became the hands of God. In ministry, we become the hands of our Host.

Inwardness becomes true substance only when we leave the table to serve in Christ's name. The French cleric Fénelon called for Christians to maintain a balance between learning and doing. He pointed out that learning rarely makes us want to do—it only breeds the desire for more learning. "We are in danger of evaluating our spiritual maturity on the basis of the knowledge we have acquired," he said.[4] In the kingdom of God, there is great compassion for the world. We are not free to hide anywhere from our responsibility—especially not in the bosom of God.

Rate the following in the order from what you would consider greatest to least as marks of spiritual maturity.

___ knowledge of the Bible
___ a servant spirit
___ understanding of theology
___ ability to teach
___ desire to be like Jesus
___ boldness to witness
___ compassion for hurting people
___ consistent prayer life
___ courage to serve in difficult places
___ humility

What traits would you add?

____

____

____

____

Francis of Assisi is a familiar example of inwardness that did not hide in God but deliberately chose to be the instrument of His peace. The true sign that Christ indwells our lives is that we turn outward to display the same kind of compassion He did. You could order the traits above in many ways, but a friend put the priority into perspective in a prayer. She said, "God, teach me to have a heart like a cathedral rather than just a mind like a concordance." Knowledge is important. Scholarship is a demand of faithfulness, but our relationships with Christ and others are most important.

Day 5 SUBMITTING TO SOVEREIGNTY

How I long for your precepts! Preserve my life in your righteousness.—Psalm 119:40

A friend who serves a rural parish has large talents, though his church is small. Yet he shows no hint of resentment that God has passed him by, giving promotions to others less talented and less educated. He seems not to notice. He has learned inner listening, and his listening life marks him as a man of rich possessions. I don't know if his active compassion for others taught him inwardness, or inwardness taught him to minister. He visits the aged who live and die with few to care for them. He touches the blind and embraces the feeble. Christ reaches through him. As I watched him one day, it seemed that I heard the Savior say, "Whatever you did for one of the least of these brothers of Mine, you did for Me" (Matt. 25:40).

How do you think Christ judges the greatness of a man's or woman's service to Him?

____

____

____

Inwardness cries with the reaching arms of Christ: "O Jerusalem, Jerusalem … How often I wanted to gather your children together, as a hen gathers her chicks under her wings" (Matt. 23:37). Certainly there is danger that others will take advantage of us. But as Fénelon said, "Happy is the one who pays no attention to his own hasty judgments nor to the gossip of others!… You must learn to despise the selfishness of your own heart, and you must also be willing to be despised by others. … Learn to draw your strength and nourishment from Jesus, and from Him alone."[5] As we serve, we may be taken for granted; but we must remember Jesus' words: "The Son of Man did not come to be served, but to serve, and to give His life—a ransom for many" (Matt. 20:28).

People continually called out for mercy when Christ was occupied with other matters. But He knew it was important to serve, even if doing so interrupted His personal agenda. Do we not shame our Lord when we refuse to be interrupted to notice the dying world around us? Someone once asked a pastor, "Do you like all the congregational interruptions in your work?" He replied, "My work is my interruptions."

Do we not shame our Lord when we refuse to be interrupted to notice the dying world around us?

Jesus came to be interrupted. This is the nature of any rescue operation, whether it be for the sick, the aged, the mentally ill, the lonely, or the spiritually lost. Jesus came "to seek and to save the lost" (Luke 19:10). These need to become the target of our ministry, as they were His.

We cannot minister as Christ did unless we can see people one at a time. We must engage in rescue work without falling into the snare of mass promotionalism. It is all too easy to be seduced into using evangelistic sales techniques. Rather, we must simply follow the lead of Christ in obedience.

How can you tell the difference between presenting the Gospel and using evangelistic sales techniques?

____

____

My own spiritual gift seems to be evangelism. Each time I open the New Testament to share Christ, I feel His strong inner approval. This is true regardless of whether those I talk with ever come to know Him. For in the very sharing of the gospel, I know obedience to the final great command of Jesus Christ to go into all the world (see Matt. 28:19).

On those occasions when I do lead others to faith in Christ, I find an overwhelming inner joy in the Holy Spirit. I have also had the more enduring joy of seeing those in Christ continue to triumph over the very needs and fears that first made them open to His love.

The Host at the table in the wilderness does not congratulate me. He does not need to. This is why I myself was born anew. He does not think I am better than others with different gifts. We glory together in the certainty that His kingdom is growing. That is a joy for both of us.

Often we mistakenly pursue the deeper life rather than obedience. But the only true evidence that we love God is our longing for obedience. Notice that the psalmist longs to obey God, not just to be in His presence. When he cries, "I long for your precepts!" he is not saying, "I just want to linger in intimate fellowship with you." He cannot demonstrate his love for God until he has done all that God has asked him to do.

What would you say to the person who says "I love God" and yet gives no evidence of a desire to obey God?

- ❑ I don't believe your faith is genuine.
- ❑ You need to grow up as a disciple of Jesus.
- ❑ God is going to get you.
- ❑ Examine yourself to see if you are in the faith.
- ❑ Other ______________________________

What does Jesus say to the issue in John 14:15?

____

____

A Bible expositor once asked his little boy to carry out the trash. His son replied to the command by saying, "Oh, Dad—you are so beautiful—you are the true giver of all things. I think I will just stay here and contemplate your face." These were nice words, but they were not obedience. In fact, without obedience we have reason to doubt the depth of admiration altogether. It is by obedience, says the psalmist, that we preserve our lives in righteousness.

Read the next paragraph carefully and answer the questions that follow.

Most people today live powerlessly. They prefer indulgence to the discipline of the table. They choose ease yet complain that they find no deep satisfaction in Christ. One hallmark of self-will is that it hungers for the fruits of obedience without the effort of attaining it.

How would you explain the phrase "the discipline of the table"?

____

____

In what sense do we face choices between self indulgence and finding deep satisfaction in Christ?

____

____

Describe a time when you chose self denial over comfort and discovered a joy in Christ that proved more than worth the sacrifice.

____

____

Did you think of times when you gave up your time to do something in the name of Jesus that you did not want to do? Or did you think of an occasion when you gave money or goods with the result that surprised you with joy?

Do you find that your self-will still continues to "hunger for the fruits of obedience without the effort of attaining it"?

❑ yes ❑ no ❑ not sure

What life principle could you write for yourself out of your experience of sacrifice leading to joy?

____

____

____

Obedience is first the candid unfolding of ourselves before our heavenly Father. Christ had no secrets from His Father. He maintained a transparent mind and conscience. So we must seek to make our lives transparent before the Father. God is ever prying the lids off of our closed minds to let in the light of His holiness, but we flee this disclosure. Foolishly, like Adam, we try to hide. Still God pursues us, crying, "Where are you?"

Refusing to be open to Him, of course, cannot shut out God's scrutiny. But our openness is a willingness to look at ourselves with Him. Repentance is not the exposure of our evil hearts, but rather the looking inward with God in weeping agreement about our condition. Here, at the end of our pride, we wait for Him to cleanse us.

Repentance is not the exposure of our evil hearts, but rather the looking inward with God in weeping agreement about our condition.

Then we are ready for submission to His will. Christ purchased His universal authority by His obedience. His life illustrates plainly that the crown of victory is forged from the gold of obedience. Likewise, our own Christlikeness is gained through our willingness to do His will. When we voluntarily come under divine command, we feel a wideness growing inside us; and when it is big enough, we can see Him there—reigning from the inner throne of our desire to obey God.

Describe a time when voluntary obedience to God created a "wideness" in you.

____

____

____

____

____

How would our lives be different if we were filled with a desire to obey God?

____

____

After we have opened to God and submitted to Him, we begin to yearn for complete identity with Christ. How could Jesus stand before Pilate in complete self-assurance? The crowd had stripped Him of His dignity, yet He gloried in His Father. Like Jesus on trial, we also gain strength by focusing on the Holy One who is our identity. We find this identity as we obey Him whose lordship is our delight. As Christ served others to please His Father, so we can minister to please Christ.

I had a friend who suffered from a disease that finally claimed his life. When he was first diagnosed, he explained, he began to separate the things that were eternal from the things that were less enduring. Like so many pastors, He had devoted most of his life to church administration and congregational concerns. He loved the things of God. But the severity of His crisis was so great that He began moving away from the "things of God" and toward God Himself. At last, he no longer prayed for healing but for identity with His Lord.

Place an X on the scale below to gauge your balance between relationship with God and involvement in the things of God?

■——————————————————■

God Himself — *the things of God*

When Helen Keller was about six years old, her aunt made a doll for her out of towels. It was shapeless and improvised, but the first thing Helen noticed when she picked it up was that the head lacked eyes. Not being able to see herself, Helen insisted that her aunt make the doll better than she was. She tugged at her aunt's string of beads and laid them approximately where the doll's eyes should have been. Her aunt touched her eyes and then the doll's head, and Helen nodded yes. The aunt found two buttons and sewed them on.

Somehow I know that quest. We are only spiritually healthy when we hunger to be better than we are.

Jesus is that hunger. We want to be made like Him, re-created in a new way to "look" like Jesus. Like little Helen, we tug at better images, crying to be remade, fashioned in an ideal form—like the very Son of Almighty God.

Christ not only identified with His Father, but He also identified with us by becoming one with us, even at the expense of death. In His dying, He was able to love and forgive His executioners because He knew who He was. In His faithful following of the whole will of God, He taught us obedience. Until we obey, the words Lord, kingdom, study, and ministry are dead. But in obedience, such words live, and we are filled with more than our pitiful, inept selves. We are filled with the holy.

---

[1]Shakespeare: The Complete Works, Vol. 1, The Comedies (London: Heron, 1900), 472-482.

[2]Jean-Pierre de Caussade, *The Sacrament of the Present Moment,* trans. Kitty Muggeridge (San Francisco: Harper & Row, 1982) 101.

[3]Bailey E. Smith, *Real Evangelism* (Nashville, TN: Broadman, 1978), 57.

[4]Fénelon, *Let Go!* (Springdale, PA: Whitaker House, 1973), 61.

[5]Ibid., 44.

WEEK 7

WIDENING OUR INTIMACY WITH CHRIST

Day 1 THE SANCTIFIED IMAGINATION

Such knowledge is too wonderful for me, too lofty for me to attain.—Psalm 139:6

One door always opens to the world of the spirit: imagination. God's realities start at the threshold of all things reasonable. Beyond begins glorious mystery, and where that mystery lies thickest, God holds His throne. The robe of God's reality is mystery. But this great mystery is why we often miss Him altogether. To follow Christ, we must make a place in our minds for God's unseen world or never confront it at all. May our imaginations serve to give us a glimpse of the glory, majesty, and mystery of God. May we create in our minds a place for the Christ of the table in the wilderness.

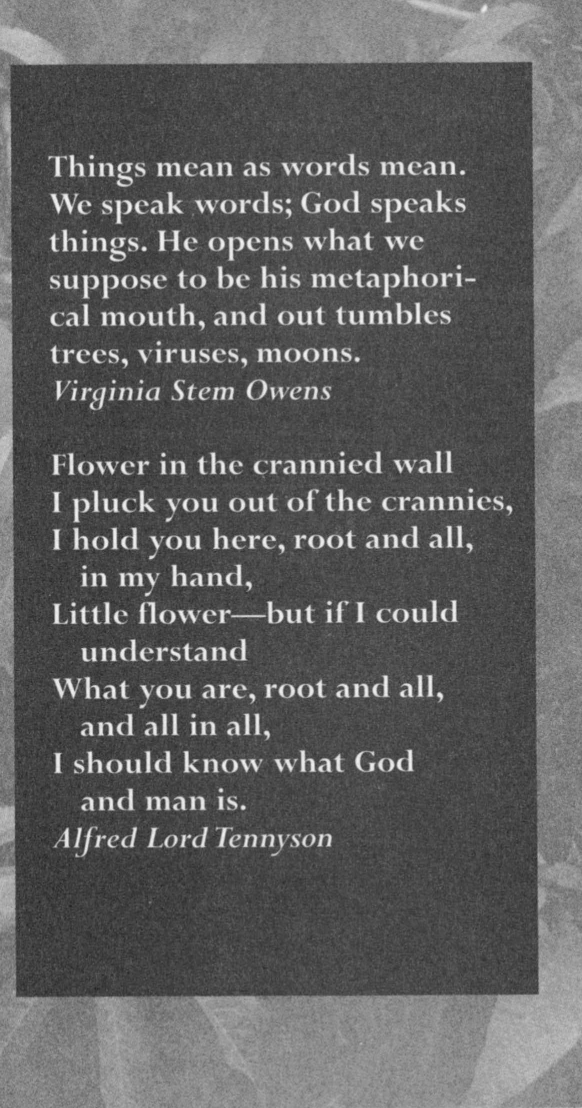

Things mean as words mean. We speak words; God speaks things. He opens what we suppose to be his metaphorical mouth, and out tumbles trees, viruses, moons.
Virginia Stem Owens
Flower in the crannied wall
I pluck you out of the crannies,
I hold you here, root and all,
in my hand,
Little flower—but if I could
understand
What you are, root and all,
and all in all,
I should know what God
and man is.
Alfred Lord Tennyson

What does Exodus 33:18-23 suggest about God's glory?

____

____

Stop and pray. Would you, like Moses, humbly ask God to show you His glory as you study today?

To take the God of galaxies and fit Him in a chair the same size as ours may seem irreverent. But size is not the important issue. A clock is not more accurate than a watch just because it is larger. We come to His table because He alone gives meaning to our world, not merely because He is big.

In Psalm 139:1-5, what knowledge do you think the psalmist considered too wonderful for himself (v.6)?

____

____

It is hard not to imagine God on a grand scale. God is vast, as are all things that attend Him. When we think of God, we think of angels and devils, harps and flames, and white thrones and gold-paved cities. Yet "love the Lord your God with all your heart" (Mark 12:30) implies that we ought also to see Him in personal terms.

How do you imagine God as He seats Himself across from you at the wilderness table for two?

____

____

____

Each of us thinks of God differently. Our inner visions are shaped by the world in which we live. In Sunday School, Black children tend to draw Black Saviors, and White children Caucasian Christs. And it's not just the imaginations we served as children. Even as grown men and women, we tend to see Christ rather like ourselves.

Still, imagination stands at the front of our relationship with Christ. We cannot commune with a Savior whose form and shape always elude us. Whenever I speak long-distance to my son or daughter, I use their voices to hang a thousand images of who they are. Likewise, in my conversations with Christ, I see Him white-robed, yet at ease in my own time. I drink the glory of His hazel eyes, thrill to the golden sunlight dancing on His auburn hair. I see His calloused hands reaching out for me and for the world He loves.

What? Do you disagree? His hair is black? Eyes brown? Then have it your way. His lordship is your treasure, as it is mine. His image must be as real to you as to me, even if our images differ. The key to vitality, however, is the image. And where did the image come from? From hundreds of books and paintings. From a thousand sermons and Sunday School lessons. The image rose from the low altar of repentance and climbed to the high altar of faith.

Bit by bit, block by imaginary block, we define Him, and we adore Him. The Bible writers did the same. Their definitions did not make God more real, but they did make His vastness more manageable for our minds.

Bit by bit, block by imaginary block, we define Him, and we adore Him.

Is it necessary to define God? Is it fair to limit the Almighty so? Is God not an ocean of infinite reality? Yes, and oceans can never be known. They are too vast. But a single drop of the Pacific can tell us the essence of all. While God's reality remains hidden, He discloses Himself to us in finiteness. This is the meaning of Christ's becoming a man.

What of those who lived and served God before Bethlehem? Abraham heard His voice: "Leave your country … and go to the land I will show you" (Gen. 12:1). What was the mental image he had of the God who spoke? We cannot know. Yet Abraham's image of God was powerful enough to motivate him to undertake a perilous journey. Abraham believed God. God was the mysterious yet powerful reality he dared not disobey.

Who appeared to Abraham in Genesis 18:1-10.

____

What significance do you see in the use of the divine name *YHWH* (signified by the English word LORD in all caps) in verses 1 and 10?

____

____

The encounter remains wrapped in mystery. When Abraham called the three men "lord" in verse 3 he used a Hebrew word that can mean simply "sir" or that could be applied even to God. But when Moses wrote the words down, he used the covenant name in verses 1 and 10.

So did God appear physically in the persons of the three visitors? I leave you to decide, but certainly when Abraham thought of God he pictured far more than an invisible force. The God of Scripture has never been impersonal. From Genesis 1 to the final chapter of Revelation, God has personhood.

Shall we go on? At a burning bush, Moses encountered the God of Abraham. How strong was Moses' mental image? So strong that he went to Egypt and stood against the greatest power in the world with a demand: "Let my people go" (Ex. 5:1). His courage must convince us—he held in his imagination a God who was sovereign.

The psalmists imagined God as a shepherd (Ps. 23), a light (Ps. 27:1), a shield (Ps. 18:2), the King of glory (Ps. 24:10), and a fortress (Ps. 91:2). Isaiah saw Him as a great, heavenly monarch, the train of whose robe filled the Temple (Isa. 6:1). John the Baptist saw Him as a harvester (Luke 3:17), Paul as a righteous judge (2 Tim. 4:8), and Jeremiah as a potter (Jer. 18:6). Each of these men, in turn, served the God whose image motivated their obedience.

What additional images grow out of ways God has worked in your life?

____

____

____

Our own devotion to God also comes from the image we hold in our minds. While Job 38:1 uses a storm or a violent whirlwind to depict God, we must not consider Job a pantheist. God is not nature. He presides above it.

God can speak to us in such a great variety of ways that we must learn to seek His mysterious reality in many ways.

- Going into Jerusalem on Palm Sunday, Jesus said that if the pilgrims and citizens of Jerusalem had not proclaimed Him Messiah, the very rocks would have done so (Luke 19:40).
- Paul said that the whole creation groaned, waiting for its redemption (Rom. 8:22).
- Isaiah even said that in the coming Zion, all of nature would be transformed so that the bear and cow would graze together, and babies would play with snakes (Isa. 11:7-8).
- Psalm 96:12 says that all of the forest will sing for joy at His coming.
- Psalm 19:1 says that the "heavens declare the glory of God; the skies proclaim the work of his hands." We must stay alert because God is ever speaking to us.

End your day's study by praising God for the many ways He shows Himself to His children. Sing or cry out to Him. Respond to His creativity with your own.

Day 2 GOD WITH US

Where can I go from your Spirit? Where can I flee from your presence?—Psalm 139:7

Even more than the natural world, God is filling all of life with Himself. Jesus said that God is Spirit, and we must worship Him in spirit (John 4:24). There is an immense wideness in this statement. God pervades the rocks and rills and hangs about us in the air. Paul reminded the Athenians that in God "we live and move and exist" (Acts 17:28). Whether we believe in God or doubt Him, we must do it from the center of God, for that is the only place we can live.

Stop to imagine the reality that surrounds you. How do you feel to realize that every moment of your life has been spent not just in God's presence but in Him?

____

____

What statements in Psalm 139 confirm that God is everywhere you could possibly ever go?

____

____

____

I have had many people tell me that they didn't see how they could ever live up to Paul's admonition to "pray constantly" (1 Thess. 5:17). But we define prayer by the image of God we hold. If we see God on a great white throne, then we see prayer as a coming and going from His presence. But if we see God as one who permeates the very atmosphere around us, then every word we speak will be heard. Every action will communicate a message to Him. All of life becomes communion, for He fills the very crannies of our minds and bodies. Even our thoughts form before His full awareness.

Let's not act as though He is somehow "out there" and that we must "go" to talk to Him.

Our world will change as we widen our view of God. We know who He is, but we also need to understand where He is. God continually accompanies us. So let's not act as though He is somehow "out there" and that we must "go" to talk to Him.

How does the awareness just described change your thoughts and feelings about prayer?

____

____

____

Most of us see our relationship with God like a marriage. We get together with God in prayer much as a husband and wife get together at the end of the day. From breakfast to supper, marriage is less "together" than when husbands and wives are physically in each other's presence.

I have heard Christians say, "We must take time for God." Or, "I get up every morning at six to pray and have fellowship with God." Or, "Between three and four is my throne time." God does preside from the great throne before the glassy sea (Rev. 4:6), and it is good to have special times focused on God. But he also stretches as far as existence itself. We must not fasten Him to some specific, faraway place and act as though we can only meet with Him there.

The marvelous Christ pervades the entire world of thought and study. We have nothing to fear, therefore, by growing in many directions at once. In fact, the more we know of psychology or literature or mathematics or philosophy, the wider our perception of God becomes.

J. B. Phillips, in his well-known book, *Your God Is Too Small,* grieved that the God of harried, busy Christians really is too small. If this is true, it is because we give Him only a fractional, religious place in our lives. As we allow God to be in charge of more of our world, our understanding of His immensity will grow. But growth can be painful. Growth demands that we step outside our religious naiveté and scrutinize the truth we were far too prone to glance over and dismiss. Many very conservative believers have a habit of boxing and filing unstated truth. I rarely find them to be wrong, only hasty and simplistic. They study truth and error only long enough to stamp it "right" or "wrong" and not "examined" or "usable."

In my youth in Oklahoma in 1950, I found it easy to be a fundamentalist. I lived on boxed doctrine. But now, pat answers and rigid categories do not satisfy the hungers of my heart. I was more certain of everything when I first knew Christ. What comfort I found in my ignorance. I had read so little and had lived such a short time that neither books nor experience blunted my clear understanding of my unstudied world. God was easy—easy as a gospel tract. I liked my easy God. He made no requirements in my little Baptist church. Oh, He preferred that I not dance or drink or go to "godless" movies. And so I didn't. What could be easier? God spoke from burning bushes and said, "No-no," and His no-no's were easily negotiated.

But all too soon, the Bible and a great many other books ruined my easy God. In widening all I knew of the world, I found answers coming slower and my assessment of people and their beliefs and relationships harder to define. But the growing made me less of a know-it-all and more prone to listen to questions, even when I had no certain answers.

We must distinguish between the essentials of the faith and the questionable matters. Mark the following either "E" for essential or "Q" for questionable.

___ the existence of God
___ the virgin birth of Christ
___ the details of the second coming
___ whether believers should drink alcohol
___ that God created and governs the universe
___ salvation in Christ alone through faith alone
___ the bodily resurrection of Christ and of believers
___ the form of government in the church

No one pays more for their faith than Christians with growing minds. For the larger our minds grow, the more we must live with an expanding volume of information that must be harmonized with the glorious simplicity of first faith. We may have responded differently to the activity above, but I hope your answers reflect one reality. We must distinguish between Christian essentials and non-essentials. When we place the expanding volume of information today against the truth of the gospel, we must beg for more light to think our universe together.

Still, God is everywhere. God literally crowds into all good books. He inhibits the theater and the laboratory. He is alive in every conversation between those He has created. God's glorious, all-pervading self awakens us to His immensity. We may celebrate Him wherever we are. He is all about us: He is the very wallboard of our offices. He is the floor and ceiling, the ground and sky of our private world. He is below the floor, above the ceiling, and beyond the wall. Wherever we walk, we push against Him and yet do not, for He swims through us, blessing us with His glorious inwardness-outwardness-upwardness-downwardness.

Then where shall we go to escape Him? The psalmist tells us it cannot be done:

O Lord, you have searched me
and you know me.
You know when I sit and when I rise;
you perceive my thoughts from afar.
You discern my going out and my lying down;
you are familiar with all my ways.
Where can I go from your Spirit?
Where can I flee from your presence?
If I go up to the heavens, you are there;
if I make my bed in the depths, you are there.
If I rise on the wings of the dawn,
if I settle on the far side of the sea,
even there your hand will guide me,
your right hand will hold me fast.
—Psalm 139:1-3, 7-10

Since God is always at hand, let us open the fissures of our being and joyously admit Him. Then we will find him leading us, following us, soaring over us, and dwelling within us. He travels with us as the companion of our journey just as He waits on the throne to greet our arrival.

Our communion with Christ is measured in two ways: We are ever in Him, yet always coming to Him. We walk in His wideness, yet we seek Him at the table.

End your days study with a time of meditation on the greatness and majesty of God. Begin by reading Psalm 93.

Day 3 GOD OF THE PARADE

If I go up to the heavens, you are there; if I make my bed in the depths, you are there. If I rise on the wings of the dawn, if I settle on the far side of the sea, even there your hand will guide me, your right hand will hold me fast.—Psalm 139:8-10

The God of Psalm 139 is the God of the noisy parade and the God of the silent wilderness. Let us discuss God in both of these categories so we may widen the boundaries of intimacy.

In which circumstance do you tend to look for God?

❑ noisy parade ❑ silent wilderness

Why do you suppose we box God into certain "religious" locations?

❑ just habit
❑ trying to show the holiness of God
❑ we've grown up thinking this way
❑ we divide life into "sacred" and "secular"
❑ the Bible teaches us to see God this way

For years, I met God only at church or in some quiet corner of devotion. How wrong I was to seek so narrowly! In Scripture we find worship at the "high places" (Ps. 78:58) more in keeping with the false gods than the God of the Bible.

Jesus lived in the streets of His day, where He saw His Father in the needy faces of those He met. In the hilarity of the moment, the all-adoring Christ took part in the laughter and the wine. The Christ of the parade was even called a glutton and a drunkard (Matt. 11:19). At dinner parties He chatted with those lucky and beloved sinners because God dwells in the thick of people. Thus, all throngs were but arenas of awakening grace. All parades were sanctified.

How can we harmonize the Christ of the good time with Christ the Redeemer? Do parades belong in the lives of Christians? Aren't they opposed to the spirit of our commitment to Christ?

How would you answer that last question?

____

____

____

In every parade I envision the crowds parting for a young rabbi seated on a donkey. Are there none in the Macy's parade to cry "Hosanna!"? Very well, then the curbstones will cry out, and the pavement itself will shout for joy. Here, where the crowd is heavy, the Savior still seeks the lost and disconsolate. God's Spirit loves the laughter, the bands, the clowns.

But those who call upon Him for salvation seldom do so at a parade. Remember Christ, looking down from the Mount of Olives upon an ancient parade—a religious festival—and lamenting, "If you knew this day what leads to peace—but now it is hidden from your eyes" (Luke 19:42). The city did not suspect that its empty merriment was observed by a wistful Savior. Yet the omnipresent God is such a lover of people that He is devoted to parades. Never in His eternal history has God missed one.

I went recently to a movie with an edifying theme. I thanked God during the film for the great artists and writers committed to noble work.

I recall a tense football game. As I viewed the coach, I remembered that he was reputed to know Christ. I thanked the Lord for him and for the game at which His own concepts of integrity marched across the football field. Did God care who won? No, unlike myself, He had not picked a team to champion. God loves both groups equally; He does not take sides. He has children on both teams. But wherever there are crowds of souls, God will be in the midst of them.

Describe a recent time when God manifested Himself to you in a non-religious setting.

____

____

____

We who contain Christ sanctify the parade. Emily Dickinson wrote:

Much Madness is divinest sense
To a discerning eye.

Once, in a crowded shopping mall, I spied a teenager sitting quietly on a rising cascade of stairs. He was alone. His eyes called me. I spoke to him. The sanctifying God had me sit, and as we spoke, our conversation turned to the young man's lonely, heavy heart.

It was not odd to find Christ in such a place. The busy mall was suddenly stilled with God's presence as we prayed together. There, in the madding throng, the parade stopped for a Sabbath moment of God's great, saving silence.

Day 4 GOD OF THE MARKETPLACE

O Lord, you have searched me and you know me. You know when I sit and when I rise; you perceive my thoughts from afar. You discern my going out and my lying down; you are familiar with all my ways.—Psalm 139:1-3

This part of the psalm makes it clear that God is familiar with all our comings and goings. He is even familiar with all of our involvement in the business world.

Just as Christ can be found in the parade, we must also allow Him in the marketplace. Too often the Christ of the wilderness table is excluded from taking any serious part in our commerce or careers. We act as though Jesus could never understand our complex world of business. Jesus seems so spiritual, and our business world seems so unspiritual.

What does Colossians 3:17,23 suggest about our attitude toward work?

____

____

We are foolish to have allowed Christ and commerce to become so separate. I have always been energized by new Christians who don't see life this way. Living in the stupor of His outrageous grace, they assume Christ is Lord of all. They refuse to let their world be divided. In the joy of their new relationship, they take their Savior into their offices and shops. Before long, vibrant Bible studies and prayer groups spring up around them. How wise they are. Until the Christ of church and the Christ of commerce are one, we have no Christ at all.

Why do you suppose we have often so separated Christ from the "real" world of work? Plan to share your thoughts in your group this week.

____

____

The Christ of the wilderness table must be allowed to sit in the company cafeteria and in the boardroom. On the faces of our fellow executives or in computer seminars, we must come to see His likeness. Is this great Christ out of place? Hardly. He once interrupted fishermen, and they left a thriving business to follow Him. He called Matthew, an internal revenue man. He spoke to politicians like Pilate on the nature of power. He called those who made a living in prostitution to seek a love more chaste.

The Christ who meets us at the table cries, "Let me go to work with you!" Psychologists and industrialists long ago discovered that much of our meaning in life comes from the hours and years we give to making a living. Therefore, we sin greatly when we make no effort to integrate Christ (who is our ultimate meaning) into our livelihoods.

Check all the ways you regularly integrate Christ into your workday and add any additional ways you can.

- ❑ talk to my non-Christian co-workers with gentleness and respect
- ❑ give thanks before eating my meals
- ❑ exercise diligence in my work so as to honor Christ
- ❑ pray for my colleagues at work
- ❑ be sensitive to meet the needs of co-workers
- ❑ develop supportive relationships with other believers
- ❑ guard my tongue against gossip or slander
- ❑ show love in tangible ways through gifts or acts of kindness
- ❑ other_______________________________________

____

____

What actions by professing believers particularly spoil their testimony?

____

____

Did you include poor work habits along with immoral living as obstacles to Christian witness? Have you noticed that sometimes the person who verbally professes to be a believer denies the faith by his or her actions and attitudes?

We must sanctify office buildings and warehouses, refineries, and assembly plants. Factories are temples too. God walks among forklifts and is desperately in love with those who wear hard hats or carry steno pads. One person I know became a Christian because someone asked Him to pray in a company cafeteria. Jesus' Great Commission can just as well be translated: Since you are going into all the world anyway, why not take the gospel with you? (Matt. 28:19).

End your study by praying for the people you work with or for people who face a challenging work situation?

Day 5 GOD OF NATURE

You created my inmost being; you knit me together in my mother's womb. I praise you because I am fearfully and wonderfully made; your works are wonderful, I know that full well.—Psalm 139:13-14

This whole psalm evokes the line from the hymn: "fairest Lord Jesus, ruler of all nature." The earlier verses exult in the perfect completion of the universe, and these verses celebrate our finished place in God's creative nature. We were specially created to be a special part of His creation.

I am most intrigued by the Christ of nature. Here the table in the wilderness ceases to be a metaphor and becomes a reality. I never love Christ more than when I meet Him in a lonely moment in the center of His natural world. Here the Christ of the table shouts His truth. His profound intimacy is a walk in the wilderness when the air is charged with God and he touches us with the glory of thunder and light. The cliffs rise and wild woods sing the song of the morning stars.

Descibe your favorite spot on the planet to celebrate the beauty of God's creation?

____

____

What makes that place special to you?

____

____

One August, I went with my wife for two days to a national monument in New Mexico. We were captivated by the majesty of the place. Rising on either side of our lodge were towering sandstone cliffs where the Anasazi (or Ancient Ones) had once lived. Now their caves were dark and silent. Here and there one could see the enduring evidence of their primeval fires. Still, there was no sound in the valley. I rose and walked the ancient ledges, dumbfounded at the display of light. The enchantment of the forest was invaded by the Christ. His fuchsia sunset blazed napalm splendor through the fiery gorge. The incandescence quickened the desert stars.

I rose before dawn and walked alone at daybreak, high upon a narrow ledge. The sun vaulted all at once above the canyon rim, and as its fire lit our world, I understood why Francis of Assisi wrote his famous *Canticle to the Sun*. "Oh Christ," I whispered, "here is my *Canticle to the Sun*—no, no, it is my Canticle to the *Son*."

Here at the table, I knew what I was—
a new creature in Christ,
born again in a love that shall outlast the sun.
Our love shall endure,

and I shall stand one million years from now
with my glorious Lover.
Then, as always, we shall be one.

In nature, God is extravagant. He declares His glory even beyond the scope of the human eye. I once hiked a deserted trail in the Grand Canyon when God's flair for color burst forth in desert flowers all around me. "Why, God?" I asked. "No one will see this shouting color. No visitor will pass on these wild, unwalked meadows."

It seemed as though God replied, "If I declare myself beyond the human senses, then let My declaration exist for the darkness and the dumb air alone. The universe has every right to applaud things not seen on the human journey."

What a pity that we do not celebrate the God of the universe for being bigger than our tiny experience. We celebrate the God of liturgy, the God of the proposition, and the God of theological excellence. Why not the God of the universal reason behind all reasons?

We can learn much about Christ in the natural world where He is so at home.

What is truly the universal language according to Psalm 19:1-3?

____

____

Circle the three people or events Psalm 19:4-5 compares.

tornado
full moon shining
figure-skater
mountain sunset
the sunrise
bridegroom
referee
lion roaring
champion at the finish line

Who is our ultimate bridegroom and champion according to Revelation 19:7?

____

We can learn much about Christ in the natural world where He is so at home. Here everything is to be sung until all the individual notes resonate with God. I see and feel the Father of my Lord. It is He who observes me, yet fills me. He sits with me and yearns to make me one with Him. Virginia Owens reminds us that "Einstein worked for three decades on his unified field theory, trying to connect gravitational and electrical fields in coherent equations. He is generally considered to have failed in this effort. But he left behind this conceptual possibility—the picture of the universe as a pulsating single organism."[1]

What does knowing that the greatest human scientists detect something uniting everything in the universe do for your faith?

____

____

Not long ago, I picked up a sego lily once from the desert floor and marveled over Jesus' proclamation: "Learn how the wildflowers of the field grow:... not even Solomon in all his splendor was adorned like one of these" (Matt. 6:28-29). I am made, and I worship by crying out, "O Lord, our Lord, how majestic is your name in all the earth!" (Ps. 8:1).

How small we keep God when we force Him to be the author of some printed devotional guide or doctrinal statement. We had better let God grow! Then we may meet Him in the art galleries of our world. There we will see the Holy One of Israel in the colored pinpoints of the impressionists or the heavy umber warmth of Rembrandt.

Were any of these artists atheists? No matter. God exists in the very threads of their canvases and will not be denied. Was the composer an unbeliever? Never mind. His unbelief will not lock God from the concert hall. Does a book we treasure as a great piece of literature not concern itself with God? Nonsense. If the book contains any beauty or makes any sense, it has come from God as surely as did Jesus. Not only has it come from God, but God inhabits its pages. We read and meet the incognito Jehovah who passes His truth from the writer's paragraphs to our retina and never mentions Himself. But if the book is full of light, it is full of God.

Mark the following statements *true* or *false* according to the previous paragraph.

___We should only read Christian books and view Christian art.

___ God reveals Himself everywhere if we develop eyes to see Him.

___We should not judge the contents of art or literature but just accept it.

What principles can guide you as you relate to the world of art and literature? Plan to discuss your answers in your group this week.

____

____

____

____

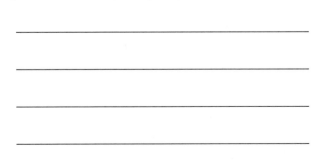

When I stop my hurrying, the God within me can hold a lively dialog with the God who is beyond me. I am too small a vessel to contain much of God. Yet crowded with His presence, I discover that I both contain and approach God at the same time. I am called from the inner altar of my private adoration to wonders that beckon me beyond the narrow borders of my spirit.

In the activity above only the second statement was true. Certainly God has called us to evaluate the messages contained in art and culture, however, we need to engage our world, not run from it. As more than conquerors, God calls us to see His majesty in all the world around us.

In a recent Christmas service, I watched a nativity scene in which a real infant played the part of the baby Jesus. The baby stretched his hand up through an opening in his blanket and there, silhouetted in the light, was a magnificent declaration. Five perfect, tiny fingers stretching and curling. The hand cried out, "Here is God ... here ... here ... here!" And the God who made the hand and declared Himself in it suddenly welled up in my own life. Saturated in His glory, He and I were enfolded into oneness. I beheld Him. Yet I couldn't behold Him, for I was one with Him and too much a part of Him to stand outside His reality to see Him. Somehow lost to myself, I knew what heaven must be. When His presence and mine become fused, I am no more, and yet more than I have ever been.

I know now the great truth of the wilderness table. I will never force the cosmic Christ into some corner where I may feed Him sour bits of church life. Nor will we meet only where the institution agrees to our meetings. He will be mine in His own music, and I will be both His song and His enthralled audience. At the table we shall talk of our love, and everywhere else we shall glory in it. Thus the intimate wilderness expands until all parades and markets join with nature to celebrate His presence and thrill to His silent and roaring reality.

[1]Virginia Stem Owens, *And the Trees Clap Their Hands* (Grand Rapids, MI: Eerdmans, 1983), 82.

Day 1 THE CORDS OF DEATH

The cords of death entangled me, the anguish of the grave came upon me; I was overcome by trouble and sorrow. Then I called on the name of the LORD: "O LORD, save me!"—Psalm 116:3-4

A prominent psychologist once said the idea that they are going to die dominates all people over thirty-five. Beyond the midpoint of our years, our gaze is focused on our headstones. We know the year of birth has already been chiseled into granite. A granite dash precedes the uncut date of our death year. We work with cardiologists and internists to extend the dash as far as we can, for we know that when the dash is done, our final date must be chiseled. The world will go on

Because I could not stop for Death,
He kindly stopped for me;
The carriage held but just ourselves
And Immortality.
Emily Dickinson

Men must endure the going hence, even as their coming hither.
William Shakespeare

This is a serious game, the defense of one's existence—how to take it away from people and leave them joyous?
Ernest Becker

beyond the final four numbers of our death date, but we will not. "Long live the granite dash," we cry, knowing all the time the dash will not endure. We shall die. It is appointed so (Heb. 9:27). As Gertrude said to Hamlet in Act I, Scene 2, "All that lives must die."

Paraphrase the verse from Psalm 116 that you would most like to choose as your motto.

____

Circle the words or phrases that best describe your feelings about dying.

can't wait *no thanks* *not interested*

good idea *painful process* *fear* *ambivalent*

in no hurry *curious* *terror* *joy*

A Beautiful Place

Mystics have sometimes described the afterlife as beautiful. But with no photographs of that remote realm—from which no visitor except Christ has ever returned—we really don't know. The prospect of taking up our residence in the land beyond obituaries frightens us.

How would you summarize your feelings about the afterlife?

____

____

Even we who know we will live "forever" are edgy. We know that dying is the prelude into life, but we like the prelude too much to get excited about the symphony to come. In Act III, Scene 1, Hamlet said it well when saying most of us would "rather bear those ills we have than to fly to others that we know not of."

A State to Fear

We also fear death because even before we yield to it, it mocks the uncertainty of life. Macbeth reprimanded the ghost of Banquo in Act III, Scene 4: "Never shake thy gory locks at me." Macbeth suffered guilt from having ordered Banquo's assassination, but he was shocked that Banquo's ghost should attend his royal dinner. After all, there was food and wine; life was beautiful. He didn't consider the idea fair that death should come uninvited to his private party. But death has a way of barging into life uninvited.

Has death barged suddenly into your family or circle of friends? ❑ yes ❑ no
If so, describe your feelings at the time.

____

____

____

____

____

____

The writer of Psalm 116 has obviously had a near-death experience. Ours is an age for such experiences, and those who have them tend to describe them in the same predictable way. As people advance into the state of death, their peripheral vision narrows to a kind of tunnel, where they see a bright light at its end. As they approach the light, they begin to feel that the light is Jesus (or God or an angel).

But in his near-death experience, the psalmist feels "the anguish of the grave" (v. 3). What he means by this term would be hard to say. Perhaps because of my claustrophobia, I see it as a closing in—that horrid sensation of being buried alive. Perhaps the psalmist feels suffocated as the finality of his life strangles him. The light is dying. The clammy fingers of death are upon his throat. He calls out unto the Almighty, "O, LORD, save me" (v. 4). The psalmist likely discovered what we all do when illness strikes and we're faced with our own mortality: Illness grimly reminds us that death is not a state but a process.

Something to be Desired

A preference for death sometimes ironically replaces the fear of death. Many suicide notes bear something of this bittersweet desire. Hamlet considered whether to be or not to be.

A physician I knew killed himself. He had spent his life caring for children with leukemia and, as he grew older, he never adjusted to the riddle of a God who loved children and yet permitted a world with diseases that killed them. Finally, after seeing so many children die, he could no longer face his inadequacy, his inability to heal. Taped to the butt of his shotgun was the short phrase, "It hurts too much to care, and it hurts too much not to care." His grieving life culminated in a grieving death. He lost the battle the psalmist insisted on winning.

I've written some of the ideas that fuel the suicide urge. Check any you've experienced or that someone you care about has expressed. Add your own examples.

❑ I'm worth more dead than alive.
❑ Others would be better off without me.
❑ My life will never get any better.
❑ I can't do anything right.
❑ Nobody will ever care about me.
❑ I just can't show my face again.

What other thoughts would you add to the list?

____

____

____

____

____

Choose one of these ideas and describe how you would counsel a depressed person to deal with such thoughts.

____

____

____

____

____

____

James Forrestal, Secretary of the Navy in World War II, was another despairing pilgrim who lost that battle. He leaped to his death from his balcony at the Bethesda Naval Hospital. His suicide note was a reflection drawn from the sad lines of Sophocles:

When reason's day sets rayless, joyless
Quenched in cold decay,
It's better to die than linger on and dare
To live when the soul's life is gone.[1]

When life is meaningless and stale, death becomes preferable. People like Forrestal, who take their own lives, see death as an acceptable way of dealing with the senselessness of life. This idea from secular existentialism teaches that life and death are endless cycles of meaninglessness.

According to the philosopher Sartre, anyone is a hero who beholds the utter futility of life and still chooses to go on living. Sartre's dour ideas are immortalized in his play, *No Exit*. Allegedly a tale of hell, it is really a tale of humankind's pointless existence and concludes that no way exists to escape from this jangling, senseless life.

What elements of our modern life do you think contribute to the tragic pessimism of so many?

____

____

____

____

The hopeful skeptics erroneously believe that death is merely opting out. Death, they say, is followed not by heaven or hell but by a pleasant, ongoing bliss that is always better than life in the here and now.

Is Hopeful Enough?

Another view of death, equally agnostic but naively hopeful, teaches that existence alone is the great good. It grudgingly accepts death as the termination of life. The famed Russian novelist Dostoevsky said that if one even had to stand on a narrow ledge with his face against a cliff for seventy years, it would be better to live like this than never to have lived at all. That may be so, but the best of all possible views is that of the psalmist. Death for him ends nothing of significance but rather is the beginning of everything valuable.

How is biblical faith different than any of the views above?

____

____

____

____

____

Day 2 ACROSS THE RIVER

The LORD *is gracious and righteous; our God is full of compassion. The* LORD *protects the simplehearted; when I was in great need, he saved me.*

—Psalm 116:5-6

When grace meets need, wonderful things happen. The psalmist affirms that God is gracious and compassionate before he declares that God has answered his despair with hope.

God had saved him.

Saved him? Saved him from what?

The fearful unknown.

But what is this fearful unknown? An escape from life? A foundless hope?

Write your own version of Psalm 116. Begin with the first verse and describe how God has delivered you.

I love the LORD, ____________________

for he heard ____________________

my voice; ____________________

he heard ____________________

my cry ____________________

for mercy. ____________________

____

____

Was the Psalmist's deliverance from death? And what is death like? Tennyson testifies to our difficulty in defining this realm in his poem "Crossing the Bar":

But such a tide as moving seems asleep,
Too full for sound and foam,
When that which drew from out the boundless deep
Turns again home.

We exhaust our imagination in trying to describe what our communion with Christ will be like when we do "cross the bar."

For tho' from out our bourne of Time and Place
The flood may bear me far,
I hope to see my Pilot face to face
When I have crossed the bar.[2]

Imagine yourself at that future moment when you first "see [your] Pilot face to face." What would you want to do at that moment?

____

____

____

____

____

We often use Tennyson's metaphor to describe death. We see death as a river to be crossed. Legend tells us that King Arthur was taken on a death barge across the murky borders of existence into the fogbound shoals that lay beyond time. The River Lethe, or Styx in

Greco-Roman literature, saw a lone, hooded figure on a barge, taking the dead across the fabled river from this world to the next.

For Christians, this river of crossing has always been the Jordan. The literal Jordan River was the final barrier to the promised land as Moses and Joshua led the people from the wilderness to the land that awaited them.

The Jordan also became the symbolic boundary between this world and the next, as in the old hymn "I Won't Have to Cross Jordan Alone":

When I come to the river at ending of day,
When the last winds of sorrow have blown;
There'll be somebody waiting to show me the way,
I won't have to cross Jordan alone.[3]

But the psalmist didn't want to cross Jordan. He had no desire to inherit the foggy, misty unknown on the far side of the river. Yet he knew that the briefness of this life is but the narrow threshold of eternity. Until this life is completely finished, we cannot speculate on the next. When poet and essayist Ralph Waldo Emerson lay dying, it is said he was urged, at the moment of his passing, to describe what he saw. But Emerson wisely replied, "One world at a time, please!"

For Christians, this river of crossing has always been the Jordan.

It's OK to prefer our side of the river. This is true even if we believe things are better on the other side. Like the psalmist, we must not be in too great a rush for eternity. We only create doubt when we speculate in our attempt to pry eternity from the mists. Certainly it is coming. Every word of Scripture seems to confirm it. Heaven is as real as Chicago. Emily Dickinson wrote:

I never spoke with God,
Nor visited in heaven;
Yet certain am I of the spot
As if the chart were given.[4]

We will survive death. The Bible contains several examples of this. The spirit of Samuel the prophet was summoned by the witch of Endor to speak of Saul (1 Sam. 28:14). In one of Jesus' parables, a rich man, enduring the torments of Hades, pleads for Father Abraham to send the dead Lazarus back to his living brothers (Luke 16:19-31).

Whether life after death exists is not so important a question as the issue of where we shall spend eternity. Those outside of Christ have often told me that they are not afraid of facing death, for in hell they will have lots of company. They have not seen hell as it is: an everlasting night of ultimate aloneness.

What do each of the following Scriptures suggest about the nature of hell?

Matthew 5:29 ________________

____

Matthew 25:41________________

____

Luke 16:23 __________________

____

What does this ultimate aloneness mean? The dark intensity of suffering always isolates the sufferer. Hell is sometimes pictured as a vast archipelago of tormented human islands. This separation of all human concourse will be ultimate. It is, in a horrible sense, the never-ending curse of a solitary confinement.

Therefore, our final crossing will elicit our crying with the psalmist, "O, LORD, save me." God will hear our cry, and our crossing the bar will be safe—our eternity secure.

End your day's study by penning a prayer thanking God for the ultimate deliverance. Seek to express the ways you are grateful for His care in this world and the one to come.

Day 3 DELIVERANCE TO UNENDING COMMUNION

Be at rest once more, O my soul, for the LORD has been good to you. For you, O LORD, have delivered my soul from death, my eyes from tears, my feet from stumbling.—Psalm 116:7-8

The psalmist exults that he has been delivered. What does he mean by this? He means that he has been allowed to go on living in this world and enjoying a longer life in communion with God. But what, after all is heaven? Paul seems to indicate in Philippians 1:21-25 that the point of all life, whether in the here and now or the there and then, is to live in ongoing communion with Christ. In fellowship with the Almighty, the psalmist says, he will no longer cry. His eyes are free of tears. He can walk without stumbling. Still, while he is in this world, he has already begun to anticipate the glory of the next world—a heightened, intimate communion with God.

Thomas Merton had a view that the loneliness of hell would come from people being repulsed by the faults in others that they know they also possess:

> *Hell is where no one has anything in common with anybody else except for the fact that they all hate one another and cannot get away from one another or from themselves.*
>
> *They are all thrown together in their fire and each one tries to thrust the others away from him with a huge, impotent hatred. And the reason that they want to be free of one another is not so much that they hate whatever they see in others as they know others hate what they see in them: and all recognize in one another what they detest in themselves: selfishness and impotence, agony, terror, and despair.*[5]

At what point does eternal life begin according to John 3:36 and 5:24?

____

Both Jesus and the psalmist indicate that eternity, be it hell or heaven, begins now. Hell is separation from God, and heaven is union with Him. Actually, either realm is merely an extension of the relationship we had or refused to have with Him while we lived on earth.

Mark the following responses *true* or *false* for you if God were to multiply your present relationship with Christ a million times over.

___ I will feel so loved by Him that I can hardly imagine the joy.
___ I presently long for such a relationship.
___ My feelings of guilt and inadequacy would surely kill me.
___ Other response ___________________________

____

The table in the wilderness is a place of unceasing relationship. Togetherness with Christ consists of more than an intermittent prayer life. Rather, it establishes a strong bridge with two piers, one driven in time and the other in eternity. The trestle of this bridge may be called death.

Paul did not contemplate suicide but rather longed for the last glorious state of foreverness. "For me, living is Christ and dying is gain. Now if I live on in the flesh, this means fruitful work for me; and I don't know which one I should choose" (Phil. 1:21-22). Paul holds within his soul an eagerness about it all. We ourselves ought to be so occupied with Christ that we walk with Him, lost in the wonder of our next estate. In the continuum of intimacy with the Savior, we anticipate in joy the boundaries of life. The indwelling presence we receive on the day of our conversion makes this hope firm. To be born again is the ultimate answer to death. Death is defeated not when we die, but when we welcome Him into our lives.

The symbols in the legend of the chart below represent key events in a believer's life. Draw a line from the symbol you choose to the life-event, or draw your own symbols.

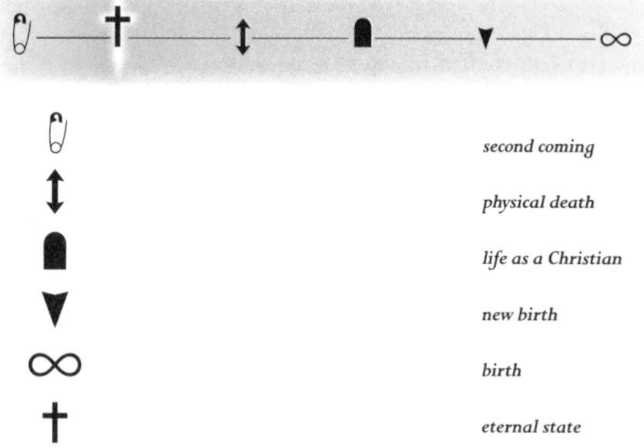

Read Ephesians 2:1-10. On the chart mark the places that correspond with the events described in verse 1, verses 4 and 5, and verse 7. You may use the verse numbers, or you may write the event such as spiritual death.

Life, as the psalmist sees it, is all of the moment. Death is not so much an ending as the beginning. Death, then, can legitimately be compared with birth. If a fetus could reason, she might argue that she did not want to leave the womb. Passing into the birth canal could crush her little form. And after all, why would she want to leave? In the womb her needs are met. She is fed without eating and lives without drawing a breath or having to protect herself from the elements. Life beyond the womb is much less certain.

But birth actually offers new levels of self-awareness and independence. The dark waters of amniotic refuge are not a haven but a prison. So foreverness in

Christ, while it is hidden, offers the promise that life is not destroyed in death but is heightened in every way.

Ephesians 2:4-5 tells us that God made us alive when we met Christ at the cross, just as the baby's life began at conception. Our present life thus represents our gestation period. Physical death or Christ's return means we finally can be born into that greater world we can no more understand now than the unborn child can understand life outside the womb.

God made us alive when we met Christ at the cross, just as the baby's life began at conception.

In Christ, all is glorious. The communion of the inward table will one day come alive with new reality. The fear of death will be displaced as a rock plunged into a pail throws out water. We become free to live in confidence. Jesus' words are realized: " 'Everyone who lives and believes in Me will never die—ever' " (John 11:26).

Though Jesus prayed in Gethsemane for deliverance from death, he did not quail in terror before it. Apart from the joyous words, "He has risen" (Mark 16:6, NIV), the second most meaningful words in the life of Christ must surely be, " 'Father, into Your hands I entrust My spirit' " (Luke 23:46). Our very passing as believers is superintended by the Father of our Lord.

We are as free of death as our resurrected Lord. Death cannot threaten us, for in the very moment of our union with Christ, eternal life became ours. Our flesh does not endure. One day our respiration and pulse will cease. But that moment will come and go and never interrupt the dynamic life that is ours. We shall claim our certain confidence with the psalmist's words: "Be at rest once more, O my soul, for the LORD has been good to you" (Ps.116:7).

A plague once swept the coast of Carthage in North Africa. Everyone feared the contagion so much that they shrank from carrying away the bodies of the dead. But a fearless band of Christians known as the *parabolani* had the courage to do this work. The *parabolani* had died to self and had no fear of what the worst contagion might do to them. The certain knowledge that death really had lost its sting in the deathless union of believers with their Lord gave them triumph over fear. Similarly, the psalmist's near-death experience had taught him that there was no need to fear changing worlds. He needed only to fear being cut off from God.

We too must die to self to free ourselves from the fear of death. In coming to Christ, Christians must take up their cross and welcome their own death to self and ambition. Since it is not possible to die twice, believers, having died ahead of death, are free. Paul said, "I consider that the sufferings of this present time are not worth comparing with the glory that is going to be revealed to us" (Rom. 8:18). Baptism symbolizes that Christians, by choice, die only once. Bonhoeffer wrote. "The baptized Christian has ceased to belong to the world and is no longer its slave. He belongs to Christ alone, and his relationship with the world is mediated through him. The breach with the world is complete. It demands and produces the death of the old man. In baptism a man dies together with his old world."[6]

How does the expectation of a greater life beyond the grave make a difference to your daily existence?

____

____

____

Day 4 NUMBERING OUR DAYS

I may walk before the LORD in the land

of the living.—Psalm 116:9

The psalmist can see now what was less clear to him before: He has been "reassigned" to the land of the living. But in sparing his life, the Almighty gave him new responsibilities in the land of the living.

We too have responsibilities in the land of the living—for the land of the living is our current address. We dare not allow our own great hope for our resurrection to lull us into spiritual irresponsibility. Our time here is brief but important. The Bible says we must be good stewards of our lives.

What does Paul the apostle tell us to do with our time in Ephesians 5:16?

____

What do the words of Psalm 90:12 add to Paul's admonition to make the most of our time?

____

These Scriptures remind me of Goya's dark painting, Saturn Eating His Children. Goya could see that time was the great devourer who fed on the world of clocks and calendars. Time eats people, and his appetite is voracious. Saturn was the god of time, and sooner or later this god devours us all.

James asked and then answered the question, "What is your life? You are a mist that appears for a little while and then vanishes" (James 4:14, NIV).

In numbering our days, we must arise each morning serious about our mathematics. With every sunrise we must subtract those days we have already spent from the total number available. Such radical calculation forces us to consider the priority of those days left to us. What are the events to which we must give our attention? To what relationships must we dedicate our remaining years? Jesus made this judgment about the prodigal son: He " 'squandered his estate in foolish living' " (Luke 15:13). It is a wasteful life that throws away the days in worthless pursuits.

When we are forced at last to leave the land of the living, all that will matter is our relationship with Christ Jesus. A busy father at last condescended to give a day of his time to his young son to go fishing. The boy never forgot the day, remembering it to the very hour of his father's death. Since it had been such an important time to the son, he eagerly leafed through his father's diary after the funeral to see what entry his father had made on that great day. He was crestfallen as he read, "The day was lost … I spent it with my son on a fishing trip!" To number our days means we are the stewards of our relationships with others.

List at least a dozen specific ways you have used your time in the last week.

____

____

____

____

____

____

____

____

Underline the activities that seemed most pressing at the time, and circle the activities that were most important in the long run.

What conclusion can you draw from the exercises you just completed?

____

____

Our fellowship at the table is the most important area of the stewardship of our days. A. W. Tozer said that we "who live in this nervous age would be wise to meditate on our lives and our days long and often before the face of God and on the edge of eternity. For we are made for eternity as certainly as we are made for time, and as responsible moral beings we must deal with both."[7]

Day 5 COMPANION SPIRIT

Precious in the sight of the LORD is the death

of his saints.—Psalm 116:15

God values believers' deaths as precious. What a magnificent commendation from a holy God! Why is the saint's death such a treasure for God? Because saints are those who used their mortality to serve the purposes of God.

Brainstorm a bit. List all the reasons you can think of why the death of a believer is precious in the sight of God.

____

____

____

____

____

I wish I could be hear your thoughts about why God values the death of His own. Many reasons could exist.

What reasons do the following Scriptures suggest?

John 17:24 _______________________________

2 Timothy 4:7 _____________________________

Revelation 12:11 ___________________________

Several times, now, I have attended the funeral of some noble man or woman of God. Always, I feel a surge of celebration. Not only had they defeated the inherent stupidity of pointless living, but they brought a state of ultimate worth to their microcosm of existence. They evangelized, healed, taught, and, in short, brought the fallen world back in the direction of the lost Eden.

The resurrection created Christianity, but the constant companionship of the Holy Spirit sustains and empowers it. Jesus promised that after He had gone away, He would send the Comforter (John 16:7, KJV). On Pentecost, the Christ of continuing presence came in the person of the Holy Spirit, the promised comfort for those who grieved the absence of the earthly Christ. The Spirit arranges our meetings with Christ at the wilderness table. And when we must at last leave the closet of this divine fellowship, the beloved Spirit walks with us into the circumstances and struggles of day-to-day living. The same Comforter enables us to deal with our own death.

Perhaps the authenticity of the Spirit's companionship is most appreciated at death. If so, the death of missionary Hudson Taylor's second wife is a demonstration of God's faithfulness. The Spirit watched between them with His presence and the assurance that no matter how much pain death brought, the separation was only temporary. J. C. Pollock's description of this event is worth noting:

> "My hair is so hot!" she [Hudson's wife] said.
>
> "Oh, I will thin it out for you, shall I?" Hudson knew she did not like to have her hair cut short because it could not be done nicely in the Chinese way.
>
> Her hair was matted and tangled with sweat. He began to cut it all off except for an inch of fuzz.
>
> "Would you like a lock of it sent to each of the three children? What message shall I send with it?"
>
> "Yes, and tell them to be sure and be kind to dear Miss Blatchly … and … and … to love Jesus."
>
> When he stopped cutting she put a hand to her head. "That's what you call thinning out?" she smiled. "Well, I shall have the comfort and you have all the responsibility as to looks. I never do care what anyone else thinks as to my appearance. You know, my darling, I am altogether yours," she said. And she threw her loving arms, so thin, around him and kissed him in her own loving way for it.
>
> Later, as the morning drew on, another conversation between Hudson and Maria began:
>
> "My darling, are you conscious that you are dying?"
>
> She replied with evident surprise, "Dying? Do you think so? What makes you think so?"
>
> "I can see it, Darling."
>
> "What is making me die?"
>
> "Your strength is giving way."
>
> "Can it be so? I feel no pain, only weakness."
>
> "Yes, you are going Home. You will soon be with Jesus."
>
> "I'm sorry …"
>
> "You are not sorry to go to be with Jesus?"
>
> "Oh no!" ("I shall never forget the look she gave me," Hudson later said, "as looking into my eyes she said:")
>
> "It's not that. You know, Darling, that for ten years there has not been a cloud between me and my Saviour." ("I know that what she said was perfectly true.") "I cannot be sorry to go to Him," she whispered. "But it does grieve me to leave you alone at such a time. Yet … He will be with you and meet all your needs."
>
> Soon after nine, the breathing sank lower. Hudson knelt down. With full heart, one of the watches wrote, he committed her to the Lord; thanking Him for having given her and for the twelve and a half years of happiness they had had together; thanking Him, too, for taking her to His own blessed Presence, and solemnly declaring himself anew to His service.[8]

How beautifully the noble pass from this world to the next. The psalmist is right: "Precious in the sight of the LORD is the death of his saints." One of these days, when our Host rises from the table, we will rise with Him and walk with Him to our last estate with His Father. It is the final step of victory and union with Christ. The fellowship will be unbroken. Just as it has been at the table, so it will ever be. For our Lord has given us His astounding pledge: " 'I am with you always' " (Matt. 28:20).

Paradise is not a narrow-gated cloister but rather an open Eden where two—the believer and Christ—may walk abreast into the final presence of God. We who live in fellowship with Christ do not approach this late hour alone.

Christ is the great rectifier of this human predicament. My mother died on an October day in 1977. She had lived for her nine children and inspired in every one of them a desire to be so much more than any of them could ever have been without her. While I was trying to sort through the folderol of funeral preparations, I was also grieving. I think I was a little angry with God. Death seemed too void of victory—too much a bleak disinheritance.

Why was I angry? Because my mother had lived such a hard life. I wondered if God had really appreciated her devotion. With little money and magnificent hardship, my mother passed away in anonymity. But my anger at her death was soon replaced by the promise of the same Comforter who filled the apostles on the Day of Pentecost.

What most encourages you about the death of a loved one you have experienced?

____

____

____

____

At his death, D. L. Moody, knowing the same confidence and fueled by the same strong comfort, is reported to have said, "Earth is receding, heaven is descending. This is my coronation day."

Death will come, but not unattended. Christ will give us His unfailing presence. We shall rise from the table in the wilderness and sit at the marriage supper of the Lamb. Intimacy will culminate in grandeur. He whom we have met so often will be the guest of honor, and all the nations will pay Him tribute—and He shall reign forever and ever. Inwardness will be transformed instantly into upwardness. And all the glory of our earthly intimacy with the Holy will be changed to an eternal, indestructible togetherness.

Write a prayer expressing to the Christ of the wilderness table your heart's feelings and thoughts about that coming togetherness.

____

____

____

____

____

In the meantime, we wait. Ours is a quiet meal. Our Host sits with us at a table whose reality holds the promise of foreverness.

---

[1]Sophocles, "Chorus From Ajax" as quoted in *The New York Times*, May 23, 1949, p. 3.

[2]W. J. Rolfe, ed., *Tennyson's Poetical Works* (Boston: Houghton Mifflin, 1898), 753.

[3]Thomas Ramsey, "I Won't Have to Cross Jordan Alone," © Copyright 1934. Renewal 1962 Broad Press. All rights reserved. Used by permission. *Hymns of Faith* (Wheaton, IL: Tabernacle Publishing, 1980), 528.

[4]Emily Dickinson, Emily Dickinson: Collected Poems (Philadelphia: Courage Books, 1991), 75.

[5]Thomas Merton, *A Thomas Merton Reader,* ed. Thomas P. McDonnell (Garden City, New York: Doubleday, 1974), 65.

[6]Dietrich Bonhoeffer, *The Cost of Discipleship* (New York: Macmillan, 1959), 257.

[7]A. W. Tozer, *The Knowledge of the Holy* (San Francisco: Harper & Row, 1961), 47.

[8]J. C. Pollock, *Hudson Taylor and Maria: Pioneers in China* (Grand Rapids, MI: Zondervan, 1970), 205–207.

LEADER GUIDE

Use the following suggestions to guide a one-hour small-group discussion of the lessons in each week's study of *A Hunger for the Holy.* Begin and end each session with prayer. The format will remain the same each week. Some questions will help members to get better acquainted. With these questions members will share elements of their journey through life. Other questions will help members to understand or apply the Scripture. Remember to share and pray together as you close.

If your group has more than eight members, consider dividing into subgroups of two to four members each for some or all of the discussion questions. You will probably not have time for all of the discussion questions. Prayerfully select the questions that best fit the needs in your group.

Ideally you will be using the accompanying video. If so, show the one-hour movie *The Psalmist* as an introductory session and enlistment aid. *The Psalmist* was made from a novella written by Calvin Miller. We recommend that you show the movie to the entire church body. Or you may show it to your specific target audience for the study.

After the movie explain that *A Hunger for the Holy* is a study based on the Psalms. Enlist members and pass out member books. Give the assignment to read and complete week 1 before the first group meeting. Each week you will have a video introduction from Calvin Miller to begin the study. The video segments are approximately 7 minutes in length and include a message from the author with a clip from the movie.

If you do not use the video kit, you can do the study from the print only. You will need to either conduct an introductory session to get people their workbooks, or get them the books and first-week assignment at the time of enlistment.

Week 1

HUNGERING AFTER THE HOLY LIFE

Before the Session

1. Complete the week 1 study in the workbook.
2. Pray for the members who will participate in your study.
3. Select from the discussion questions those that you think will be meaningful for your group. Prepare your own questions as needed.

During the Session

1. Check roll as members enter.
2. Use name tags if members do not know one another well.
3. Begin with prayer.
4. Read Psalm 1. Ask members to each share what aspect of the Psalm most appeals to them. Ask the first time they can remember hungering after a holy life. Show the video segment for week 1.
5. Select from the following the questions you will discuss as a group. You may want to divide into smaller groups so members will have adequate time to share. Never force members to share, but provide them opportunities to participate.
   - Share with the group one of the three life experiences that have most made you face your inner self (p. 7).
   - Ask members to share their definitions of repentance (p. 7). Make notes on tear sheets or marker board. Lead the group to develop their own definition of repentance.
   - Ask class to divide into pairs or groups of thee. Have them share: "How was your salvation experience similar to and different than the author?"
   - Ask: "What do you think Calvin Miller means on page 12 when he said that outwardness is good but easily spoiled?
   - What practical warning signs point to hypocrisy (p. 14).
   - Ask members to discuss in their small groups how great a challenge they find it to quiet their mind and spend time alone with Christ (p. 15).
   - How can we distinguish between our own feelings for Jesus and Jesus Himself? (p. 18). Answers should include balance devotion with serious study because Scripture is our authority for understanding Jesus.
   - Ask group members to share their desires for growth (p. 19).

6. Close with prayer for yourself and members to grow to hunger and thirst righteousness. Remember that Jesus is the righteousness of God.

After the Session

1. Evaluate your group experience. Did everyone participate in the group discussion? Did one or more members dominate the group? Did you allow members to be involved in the session?
2. Plan changes you will make before leading the next group meeting.
3. Contact each member of the group sometime during the week. Encourage them to complete their Bible study daily.
4. Pray for each group member by name each day this week.

Week 2

BARRIERS TO THE INWARD JOURNEY

Before the Session

1. Complete your study of the daily assignments.
2. Review the suggested group discussion questions.
3. Prayerfully plan how you will lead the group discussion.
4. Remember to pray for each member. Ask God to give you sensitivity to their personal and specific needs.

During the Session

1. Check roll and greet members as they enter. Use name tags if members do not know one another well.
2. Begin with prayer.
3. Together read Psalm 51. Show the video for week 1.
4. Choose from the following discussion questions and activities.
   - Read John 4:32. Relate that Jesus had just been talking with the woman at the well. Ask members what they think Jesus meant that He had food to eat they knew nothing about? Ask how Jesus statement in John 4:32 relates to the suggestion that "the Host is our meal" on page 21.
   - Ask, "How do the excesses of 'junk-food Christianity' described on page 22 distract us from intimacy with Christ?"
   - Discuss the statements from page 23: "God created us to be receptacles of Himself, but in spite of the Holy Spirit's readiness to invade our

lives, most of us hold nothing. Our inner lives—created by God to contain Himself—hold only little trinkets—the tinsel of our egos."

- Ask, "How does our ego take the place of worshiping Christ?" (see p. 24, shallowness)
- Lead a discussion of the question: "Why doesn't legalism solve the problem of sin?" (p. 26). Compile a list of reasons for the failure of legalism to create genuine holiness. Follow up with the question, "How can worship do what legalism cannot?"
- Ask members to share their response to the question on page 27: "What is the difference between sacrificing for Christ and adhering to legalistic rules?"
- Lead a discussion of fasting. First brainstorm a list of behaviors from which people could fast. You might point to 1 Cor. 7:5 as a biblical example. Then discuss the possible benefits and dangers of fasting.
- Discuss the question on page 30: "What kinds of pressures urge us to abandon our ideals as we go through life?
- Discuss how a sense of entitlement grows in our lives (p. 32).
- Discuss the difficulty presented by our hurried lives. Ask how members can clear their minds of distractions and focus on Christ (p. 34).

5. Close the discussion with a time of praying for one another.

After the Session

1. Spend a few minutes reviewing the session. Make notes in the margin. How did the session go? Did all or most of the members take part in the discussion? Did the group stay on task, or did they stray onto topics that had nothing to do with the study? What do you think you can do to improve your group leadership skills and the group experience next week?
2. Pray daily for each member of the group. If you sense particular needs, pray specifically for God's ministry in those areas.
3. Make some contact this week with each group member to encourage them in their study. Send a card, make a phone call, or make a point to briefly drop by to see them.

Week 3

THE NEEDLE'S EYE

Before the Session

1. Plan the discussion questions and activities you will use.
2. Consider how you can be creative in leading the session. Be certain you have allowed the subject matter to work in your life before you attempt to lead others.

During the Session

1. Greet members.
2. Begin with prayer.
3. Read Psalm 37. Show the video for week 3.
4. Select from the following group discussion activities.
   - What situations tempt you to envy those who ignore God and yet seem to prosper (p. 38)?
   - Brainstorm as a group and make a "lizard list" (see page 38).
   - Divide into two groups. From page 41, have one group make a list of ways to strengthen our grip on Christ and the other group make a list of ways to loosen materialism's grip on us.
   - Discuss how it feels to know the smile of God because you've put Him first (p. 42).
   - Ask members to share what lesson they drew from the testimony of Thomas à Becket?
   - Discuss the question on page 45: "Do you think we are more tormented by what we have or what others have that we don't?
   - How would it feel to be totally free from the concern to "keep up with the Joneses?" (p. 46).
   - What makes the difference between the two types of people in the activity on page 48?
   - What would you say to a friend who was disappointed with God?
5. Conclude the session with opportunities for members to share their testimonies of dealing with this issue. Pray for each other.

After the session

1. Review the session in preparation for next week.
2. Pray for the needs of each group member each day this week.

Week 4

THE UNFORSAKING CHRIST

Before the Session

1. Plan the discussion questions and activities you will use.
2. Remember that the best teaching is confessional. Do not dominate the group but do share your heart as an example for the group members.

During the Session

1. Greet members.
2. Begin with prayer.
3. Read Psalm 22. Show the video for week 4.
4. Select from the following group discussion activities.
   - If you have experienced a time when God seemed silent, what was the most difficult part of that time? (p. 51)
   - What songs speak to you of Jesus' friendship and humanity? (p. 54)
   - Ask members to compile a list of why problems sometimes become all consuming (p. 55).
   - How does it feel when it seems that God is blessing those who have harmed you or someone you love? (p. 56)
   - Ask members to list all the ways life would look different from the vantage point of heaven (p. 57).
   - Ask: "If you could write back from heaven, what advice do you think you would give yourself for now?" (p. 58)
   - How would it change life if we could avoid all temptation to compare ourselves with others? (p. 59)
   - What shortcomings in your life might you have never seen if you were not confronted by them in the lives of others? (p. 60)
   - Ask: "Have you experienced a time when fear grew larger and 'camped like a wall of demons' between you or someone you love and Christ'?" If so, how did it feel, and how have you learned to overcome those feelings? (p. 62)
5. Conclude the session with prayer.

After the Session

1. Note in the margin the actions you can take to improve class participation and learning next week.
2. Pray for each group member this week.

Week 5
THE HOLY COMMUNION OF PRAYER

Before the Session
1. Review the week's study and plan your discussion questions.
2. Pray for the leadership of the Holy Spirit for yourself and the group.

During the Session
1. Greet members.
2. Begin with prayer.
3. Read Psalm 42. Show the video for week 5.
4. Select from the following group discussion activities.
   - How do you think a person can balance busy-ness and time alone with God? (p. 65)
   - Why do you think a loving God would allow times when we seem unable to reach Him? If you have gone through such a time and come out the other side, what treasures did you find in the darkness? (p. 67)
   - What moral did you write for the story on page 69?
   - How would you distinguish between acting like God's advisor and worshiper? (p. 70)
   - What does Jesus seem to mean by "glorifying" His Father in John 17? (p. 71)
   - What can you do to improve your communication with God? (p. 72, 74)
   - What kinds of chatter do you have to deal with most in the thoroughfare of your mind? (p. 74)
   - Discuss the benefits of personal rather than formalistic prayer (p. 75).
   - Discuss the exercise in "Christifying" from page 77. Invite members to share their lists.
5. Conclude the session by leading the group to compile a list of things God has taught them this week. Spend time thanking Him for His leadership and ministry.

After the Session
1. Have any group members been absent or dropped out of the class? Contact them this week to show love and concern.
2. Review the group session. Make notes in the margin of needs to pray for and lessons learned.
3. Daily pray for each member of the group by name and by need.

Week 6

WALKING IN OBEDIENCE

Before the Session

1. Select from the discussion questions those you will use.
2. Pray for the specific needs of your group members.

During the Session

1. Begin with prayer.
2. Read Psalm 119:33-58. Show the video introducing week 6.
3. Select from the following group discussion activities.
   - What would be the difference between believing truths and entering a relationship with Christ? (p. 79)
   - How do you think your life would be different if you totally delighted in God's authority? (p. 80)
   - Ask members to divide into pairs and share their areas of freedom and of temptation from page 82 (fear, worry, greed, and lust). Instruct them to pray for each other that they may grow in faithfulness and freedom.
   - How would you explain to your child the importance of rigorous rather than casual obedience to the commands of God? (p. 83)
   - Why does being a follower of Christ demand a lifetime of seriously studying God's Word? (p. 84)
   - What benefits do you think can come from having your heart turned toward God's law? (p. 85)
   - How do you think Christ judges the greatness of a man's or woman's service to Him? (p. 87)
   - How can you tell the difference between presenting the Gospel and using evangelistic sales techniques? (p. 88)
   - Discuss a time when you chose self denial over comfort and discovered a joy in Christ that proved more than worth the sacrifice (p. 89).
   - Describe a time when voluntary obedience to God created a "wideness" in you (p. 90).
   - How would our lives be different if we were filled with a desire to obey God? (p. 90)
4. Invite each member to participate in a time of sentence prayer to conclude the session.

Week 7
WIDENING OUR INTIMACY

Before the Session

1. Prepare the discussion questions and activities you will use this week.
2. Review the week's study and the entire group experience. Begin to think of how to conclude the group and to bless the members as they continue their spiritual journeys.

During the Session

1. Begin with prayer.
2. Read Psalm 139 and show the video for week 7.
3. Select from the following group discussion activities.
   - How do you imagine God as He seats Himself across from you at the wilderness table for two? (p. 93)
   - Review the ways the Psalmists described God (p. 95). Do you have any additional ways of seeing God from your life experience?
   - How does the awareness of God's presence in every aspect of life impact your thoughts and feelings about prayer? (p. 96)
   - How do you determine what is essential to the faith and what is questionable? (p. 97) What questionable issues do you have the greatest difficulty accepting?
   - How do you harmonize the "Christ of the good time" with "Christ the redeemer"? (p. 98)
   - Why do you think we've so often separated Christ from the "real" world of work? (p. 100)
   - What makes your favorite spot to meet with God special to you? (p. 101)
   - What principles can guide you as you relate to the world of art and literature? (p. 103)
4. Invite group members to reflect over the weeks study. Ask them each to share one meaningful message they have gained from one of the Psalms you have studied.
5. Close with a prayer of thanksgiving.

After the Session

1. Plan how you will conclude the study next week. You may want to plan a celebration. Use your creativity.
2. Make a personal contact with each group member this week.

Week 8

FOREVERNESS

Before the Session

1. Conclude your plans to bring closure to the group. Make the closure a time of celebration to complete your group experience. You may want to eat a meal together or go on a field-trip. The focus of the study has been to expand your relationship to Christ, so exercise your creativity in choosing a way to conclude the group.
2. Plan to personally express your appreciation to each group member.

During the Session

1. Begin with prayer.
2. Read Psalm 116 and show the final video segment.
3. Share your affection and encouragement with the group. Thank them for their diligence and faithfulness
4. Select from the following group discussion activities.
   - Describe your feelings at a time when "death barged suddenly" into your family or circle of friends (p. 106).
   - What thoughts do you think fuel people's suicide urge? (p. 106)
   - Offer members an opportunity to share their version of Psalm 116 (p. 108).
   - What would you want to do when you "see your Pilot face to face"? (p. 108)
   - How does the expectation of a greater life beyond the grave make a difference to your daily existence? (p. 112)
   - Brainstorm as a group. List all the ways you can of why the death of a believer is precious in the sight of God (p. 114).
   - What most encourages you about the death of a loved one you have experienced? (p. 116)
   - To what do you look forward most in heaven?
5. Conclude the group in the way that you have planned.

May God richly bless you for participating in and leading this study of God's Word.

ARE YOU HUNGRY?

We humans are a hungry lot. Whether we recognize it or not, we all have a deep spiritual yearning for a power beyond ourselves—a yearning that nothing but our Holy God can satisfy.

Through a study of the Book of Psalms, Calvin Miller explores our hunger for intimacy with God. In *A Hunger for the Holy*, group members will explore such topics as: Hungering after the Holy Life, Barriers to the Inward Journey, and Widening Our Intimacy with Christ.

A Hunger for the Holy: Nurturing Intimacy with Christ offers a special feature—the optional leader kit provides *The Psalmist,* a movie based on a novella by the author. Perfect as preparation for the group, the movie can also be used to promote the study beforehand or as a community outreach event. The optional leader kit also contains segments with Calvin Miller for each group session.

A Hunger for the Holy resources include:
Leader Kit Contains two DVDs that hold the eight group video sessions and the movie The Psalmist, and one copy of the Member Book. Group video sessions feature the author Calvin Miller. ISBN 0-6330-9146-4
Member Book Includes daily individual study material and leader helps. The study can be conducted either with or without the supporting video. ISBN 0-6330-9934-1

ISBN 0-6330-9934-1
9 780633 099343